COVER PHOTO

A settler harvests rice at K-18 Village, near Dyabali, about 200 kms north of Segou, Mali. K-18 is one of the villages built by the "Office du Niger" on land reclaimed for intensive rice cultivation with the support of the World Food Programme. WFP photo by F. Mattioli.

FOOD AID
and
POLICY
for
ECONOMIC
DEVELOPMENT

An Annotated Bibliography and Directory

by

Melissa Lawson Cadet

Trans Tech Management Press

© Copyright 1981 by **Melissa Lawson Cadet**

All rights reserved. No part of this work may be reproduced or translated in any form, by print, photoprint, microfilm or any other means without written permission from the publisher.

Library of Congress Card Catalog No. **80-53500**

ISBN - Hard: **0-938398-00-8**
ISBN - Soft: **0-938398-01-6**

TRANS TECH MANAGEMENT PRESS
P.O. Box 23032
Sacramento, California 95823

FORWARD

Over the past decade, economists, agricultural development specialists, food policymakers, government officials and development planners fervently debated the relationship between food and development. The 1974 World Food Conference reflected the culmination of international concern about countries unable to feed their populations. A key issue of the discussion was the role of food aid. As the number of food-deficit nations increases, the demand for food aid grows but the supply diminishes. Even if food aid were available in sufficient amounts, does it contribute to the country's development or to further impoverishment of the rural poor? The resolution of this controversy will command very wide interest in the decade of the eighties.

The number of theoretical and empirical contributions to the literature appearing after 1964 increased tremendously. Yet, their interdisciplinary nature often made them difficult to locate. This annotated bibliography -- the only one in its field covering the sixteen year 1964-1980 period -- should prove helpful to those conducting research and preparing general studies in the field. It pulls together a wide variety of books, journals, United States government and international publications and includes many more helpful resources such as the Food Aid Directory and Author's Guide explained in the Preface.

This work will make it easier to place future food aid and food policy studies in the broader context of development. Additionally, I hope those who use this book will find it saves them numerous hours of research work.

Melissa Lawson Cadet
January, 1981

PREFACE

Food aid generally applies to foreign assistance efforts undertaken to provide food on a less than commercial basis or to foster food production and agricultural development. It is viewed as an interim measure until the recipient country can become self-sufficient in food production, or, where national self-sufficiency is not a realistic prospect, until the country can meet the costs of necessary food imports from its own resources. Food aid is a short term response to complex issues conditioning food availability. It temporarily relieves a food production and food distribution bottleneck, but it does not always lead to development. At best, food aid is a transfer device -- a mechanism for moving food from surplus areas to deficit ones. At worst, food aid could lead to dependency -- an undesirable consequence of over-reliance on external food assistance. Nevertheless, food aid can be used constructively to promote desirable long term goals such as greater food supplies, more balanced economic growth, and the reduction of rural poverty and unemployment.

Since underdeveloped countries will need about two and one-half billion dollars worth of food aid annually to meet their minimum need in the next decade, actual or potential denials of food aid are key factors influencing the nutritional and, less directly, developmental fate of many underdeveloped nations. Development, traditionally viewed in the economic sense, is generally associated with an increase in productivity. However, in recent years, development has been given a new mandate incorporating the view that it should not only be associated with productivity increases and the adaptation of modern technology, but should also focus on the ability of the poorest people in the poorest countries to meet their basic human needs on self-sustaining bases. For instance, recent foreign aid legislation of the United States Congress emphasizes that, ". . . assistance shall be to support the efforts of less developed countries to meet fundamental needs of their people for sufficient food, good health, home ownership and decent housing, and the opportunity to gain the basic knowledge and skills required to make their own way to a brighter future." Additionally, future development prospects of food-deficit nations will depend crucially on agriculture since most of their labor force traditionally depends on this sector for subsistence and productive employment.

Scope of This Bibliography

This bibliography assembles a variety of published works which define relationships between food aid, food policy and development. Particular emphasis is placed on the role of food aid. Does it assist or retard the development planning effort? Since food aid may take up about fifty percent of the slack caused by shortfalls in staple food production, it is important to define and assess the linkage between food aid and economic development, particularly agricultural development. For example, in 1970, African countries began importing fifteen to twenty million tons of major staple foods annually -- half of which was in the form of food aid. Answers must be sought to such questions as: Under what conditions will the availability of food aid help relieve a country's pressing claims on foreign exchange? How will it affect future debt servicing or imports of other agricultural or intermediate goods? Will the increasing reliance on food aid reduce incentives for domestic agricultural production? Can the concentration of agricultural surpluses and food aid in the hands of the United States, Canada and a few other countries lead to volatile food pricing policies and instable supplies resulting in market uncertainty and even high prices? Does the acceptance of food aid affect domestic agricultural development policies? Can a food aid program be linked to nutrition by ensuring that the poorest groups increase their consumption and productivity? These are only a few of the topics discussed and debated in the published works included in this bibliography.

Time Period

The period covered is the past sixteen years from 1964 to 1980 -- a time during which most food aid programs reached their highest peaks of activity. Greater emphasis is placed on the theoretical and empirical studies of recent years.

Sources

Sources of information include books, periodicals, magazines, journals, government and international publications, and pamphlets. It also includes some draft reports and typewritten manuscripts of non-governmental organizations and recognized scholars in the field. Many of the writers are American or British.

How to Use This Book

This book is divided into three major components. First, the annotated bibliography consists of 445 entries arranged in alphabetical order by the author. The annotations provide a summary of the main conclusions or findings of the study or article in most cases. They give the researcher an indication of the context and level of the discussion. They are not complete summaries of the publication.

The second part, the Author's Guide, provides the most recent information about the author at the time of publication. It facilitates increased communication among scholars and government personnel with similar or opposing points of view and may also act as a guide to the credibility and reliability of the author's work.

The third part, the Food Aid Directory, lists the names and addresses of international non-governmental organizations, private or governmental organizations by country, United States government and voluntary organizations, and United Nations System and Intergovernmental Organizations. The Directory also contains a brief description of the food aid activities and publications of each agency.

Finally, each entry is cross-indexed. Entries are numbered consecutively and the subject index numbers refer to entries, **not** to pages.

Acknowledgements

Grateful acknowledgement is made of the invaluable assistance and encouragement of my husband, Max-Henri, and the help of the United Nations Food and Agriculture Organization, the World Food Programme, librarians and library staff of the University of California, Davis.

Melissa Lawson Cadet
Ph.D. Candidate, Agricultural Economics
University of California, Davis

CONTENTS

FORWARD
PREFACE

Page

I. **ANNOTATED BIBLIOGRAPHY** 1
   Bibliographies 1
   Listings (entries) 2

II. **AUTHOR'S GUIDE** 115

III. **DIRECTORY OF FOOD AID AND DEVELOPMENT AGENCIES** 126
   International Non-Governmental Organizations 126
   Private or Government Organizations by Country 129
   United States
       Government Organizations 134
       Private, State and Voluntary Organizations 139
   United Nations Systems 154

IV. **SUBJECT INDEX** 167

V. **LIST OF ABBREVIATIONS** 177

ANNOTATED BIBLIOGRAPHY

BIBLIOGRAPHIES

1. HENDERSON, Elizabeth Wilhelm. <u>Food Aid: A Selective Annotated Bibliography on Food Utilization for Economic Development.</u> Rome: FAO 203 p.

    1964

    Sponsored by the WFP, this bibliography includes 404 entries "dealing with all, and especially long-term, aspects of the present and prospective supply (encouragement and/or prevention), disposal and utilization of surplus products with special reference to food and to development aid." Background material and basic texts of special relevance, such as laws, major development plans, international agreements, are copiously indexed. The period covered is 1954-1964.

2. RECHCIGL, Miloslav Jr. <u>World Food Problem: A Selective Bibliography of Reviews.</u> Cleveland, Ohio: CRC Press 1975. 211 p.

    1975

    This publication provides an authoritative and comprehensive bibliography on important facets of the world food problem, encompassing such questions as the availability of natural resources, the present and future sources of energy, population growth, food aid, food and nutrition policies, agricultural and industrial aspects of food production, and information on the production of specific crops and animals. References on the state of world food and nutrition in specific countries are also provided.

LISTINGS

3.   ADCOCK, Robert E. "P.L. 480 Research Stresses Pest Control and Marketing." *Foreign Agriculture* 6 (1): 6-8, January.
1968

Discusses fiscal year 1967 grants for agricultural research projects under Title I of P.L. 480 made to 16 foreign countries. The projects ranged from study of the hairy sprout potato disease to experiments with animal food production. Thirty percent of the 1968 awards dealt with insect control. Evaluates the results and potential findings of these projects.

4.   AGRICULTURAL DEVELOPMENT COUNCIL, INC. "Implementation of United States Food Aid -- Title III." Report No. 20.
1979 New York: Agricultural Development Council, Inc. August. 8 p.

A summary of ideas and suggestions raised during a January 15-16, 1979 seminar on Implementation of United States Food Aid. Discusses the role and impact of food aid with respect to the following issues: 1) effects on product prices and food production policies; 2) income distribution effects; 3) development impacts, including effects on the balance of payments; and 4) expansion of U.S. farm products. Highlights various aspects of food aid policy and a number of points on which agreement in the seminar was strong. Some seminar recommendations are: 1) There is a critical need for U.S. staff who are knowledgeable, well-informed, sensitive, and perceptive about countries receiving food aid and about food assistance problems; 2) The institutional capacity to plan and administer food aid programs in recipient countries should be developed; and 3) Policies on prices and related matters should be central considerations in designing food aid activities and related development efforts.

5.   AHMED, Raisuddin. *Foodgrain Supply, Distribution, and Consumption Policies Within a Dual Pricing Mechanism:*
1979 *A Case Study of Bangladesh.* Washington, D.C.: International Food Policy Research Institute. 82 p.

Provides a quantitative framework for the discussion of food policies in Bangladesh influencing 1) effective demand for food; 2) better management of the food system; 3) food imports; and 4) nutritional status. Examines the relative efficiency of price support and fertilizer subsidy policies to increase rice production.

6. AMERICAN ENTERPRISE INSTITUTE. "A Conversation with Anne de Lattre." Developing the Sahel. Washington, D.C.: American Enterprise Institute for Public Policy Research. 19 p.

1979

Anne de Lattre is a political economist. Her specialty is economic development aid and development policy of the OECD. She is head of the secretariat of the Club du Sahel. She explains that the principal objective of the Club du Sahel is "greater food security, as the basis for more diversified development." She also describes the organization's approach toward the sensitive issue issue of cereals price policy in the Sahel.

7. AMIN, Galal A. Food Supply and Economic Development. London: Cass, 132 p.

1966

Brief discussion of the dangers of food aid with respect to the cases of India, Pakistan and Egypt. Contends that: 1) the disincentive effect of food aid on agricultural production has been exaggerated (based on the experience of India and Pakistan); and 2) an increase in the flow of food aid may actually benefit the recipient's agricultural production based on the case of Egypt. Provides no theoretical framework for the analysis of the impact of food aid on agricultural development.

8. ARNOLD, Adlai F. Foundations of an Agricultural Policy in Paraguay. New York: Praeger Publishers. 294 p.

1971

A case study of the underlying factors affecting agricultural development in Paraguay. Includes a discussion of the country's agricultural policies and development plans from 1537 to 1973 and suggests approaches to enhance the agricultural development of the country. Concludes that the greatest obstacle to agricultural development is rooted in land tenure.

9. ARROYO, Gonzalo. "Agriculture and Multinational Corporations in Latin America." In The Political Economy of Food, pp. 176-214. Edited by Vilo Harle. Farnborough, Hants, England: Saxon House, Teakfield Ltd.

1978

Clarifies the role of multinational corporations in agricultural development. Provides examples of constraints to the implementation of food production policies in Latin America, and the effects of such policies on production and food consumption.

10. AYERS, Alvin D. "P.L. 480 Rupees Support Agricultural Research in India." *Foreign Agriculture*, 4 (52): 3-4,
1966   December.

Discusses the acquisition of nonconvertible rupees from the sale of Title I P.L. 480 food aid to India and their support of its research. In 1966, India had the largest of all P.L. 480 research programs. Describes the accomplishments of these projects and their value to the U.S.

11. BANDYOPADHYAYA, Kalyani. *Agricultural Development in China and India*. New Delhi, India: Wiley Eastern. 204 p.
1976

Analyzes the process of agricultural development in China after the revolution and in India after its independence. Compares the food production performance of these nations during the past 25 years.

12. BARD, Robert L. *Food Aid and International Agricultural Trade: A Study in Legal and Administrative Control.*
1972   London: Lexington Books. 321 p.

Addresses "aspects of the economic and financial interrelationships between food aid and international agricultural trade that may be affected through control methods fitting a broad definition of law." Analyzes the impact of various food aid practices upon commercial trade according to "specific conduct rules and procedures for administering these rules." The analysis proceeds on five levels: 1) "identifying the range of objectives attributable to a given food aid donor; 2) determining the extent to which these are internally consistent or conflicting; 3) establishing criteria for ranking or ordering these objectives; 4) measuring the degree to which various food aid transactions may achieve given objectives; and 5) evaluating the effectiveness of each potential legal/administrative control device in eliminating unwanted or undesirable side effects of uncontrolled food aid." Also describes "standards and procedures now employed or seriously proposed to regulate the impact of food aid upon commercial agricultural trade."

13. BELDEN, Joe and FORTE, Gregg. *Toward A National Food Policy* Washington, D.C.: Exploratory Project for Economic Alter-
1977   natives. 228 p.

Advocates the food policy position of the Exploratory Project for Economic Alternatives. Discusses structural weaknesses in U.S. agriculture, price policy, farm exports,

-4-

and agricultural trade controls. Condemns the dominance of the agri-business complex and its collusion with government and corporate power. Claims that: "consumers, small farmers, nutritionists, environmentalists, workers and community-control activists can find a unity of interest in achieving low food prices and a decentralized, safe, and ecologically sound food production and marketing system."

14. BELL, Richard E. "U. S. Food Aid Down in 1974, May Rise Somewhat in 1975." *Foreign Agriculture* 12: (18): 9-10,
1974 May.

Explains the 50 percent reduction in P.L. 480 exports from fiscal 1973 deliveries. Some of the reasons were: 1) increased grain production in many developing countries; 2) increased food aid from Australia, Canada, the European Community and Japan; 3) the tight demand/supply situation and increases in domestic food prices; and 4) the priority given to Title I food exports to Vietnam and Cambodia.

15. BERG, Elliot. *The Recent Economic Evolution of the Sahel.* Ann Arbor, Michigan: Center for Research on Economic
1975 Development. 247 p.

A lucid analysis of the myriad problems of drought in West Africa. Chapter V discusses the "Food Subsidy Catastrophe" of Mauritania, Senegal, Mali, Upper Volta and Niger. Provides specific food subsidy policy information for each country. The author concludes that "These costly subsidy policies had profoundly negative effects: transfer of resources from potential developmental use to current consumption; redistribution of income from export crop growers to largely urban consumers, with consequently negative incentive effects on production as well as dubious equity implications; stimulation of smuggling; and stimulation of consumption of imported grains (rice) as against local sorghum and millet. Briefly discusses food aid contending that it 1) mitigated the impact of drought; and 2) provided a much-needed source of food imports on concessional terms.

16. BERGASSOLI, Michel. "Scope and Conditions for Improved Use of Food Aid for Development: The Case of Niger." In
1978 *Food Aid for Development*, pp. 69-82. Edited by Hartmut Schneider. Paris. Development Centre of the OECD.

Study of the impact of food aid in Niger from 1972 to 1977. Discusses the trade-offs between emergency food aid and development food aid. Contends that "all emergency aid should be converted into project-related food aid." Other topics discussed include the use of food aid to buy fertilizer, the determination of the food aid need, grain shortage, food aid distribution and food aid and urban consumption.

17. BERGESEN, Helge Ole. "World Food Negotiations: An Assess- of Development on Crucial Issues." In The Political Economy
1978 of Food, pp. 23-46. Edited by Vilo Harle. Farnborough, Hants England: Saxon House, Teakfield Ltd.

Focuses on the working of the world economic and political system with regard to the distribution of food and international management and administration of world food policies. Discusses two policy approaches to the food problem: the growth policy approach and the redistribution approach. Issues of food self-reliance and dependence are raised. The author contends, "In the absence of sufficiently capable IR's (international regimes) in world food policy, increasing interdependence will be a destabilizing factor, raising a life and death issue, the distribution of food, to a global level where it becomes unmanageable. If there is no breakthrough in the difficult negotiations on world food policy and on effective IR to implement it, the global food market will continue to be dominated by the most powerful nations."

18. BHATTACHARJEE, J.P. "Population, Food and Agricultural Development: A Medium-Term View." Food Policy 1 (3): 179-
1976 191, May.

Discussion of the interrelations of population with food and agricultural development. The author focuses on accelerating increases in food production and calls for an equitable and efficient distribution particularly among the poorer sections of the population; increasing employment in agriculture and related sectors; and increasing the share of developing countries in expanded trade in agriculture products.

19. BLYTHE, Colin. "Norwegian Nutrition and Food Policy: Consumer Information and Price Policy Aspects," Food Policy
1978 3(3); 163-179, August.

Discussion of the underlying goals and effectiveness of the Norwegian Nutrition and Food Policy by highlighting specific governmental actions. Focuses on two aspects of the policy: consumer information and price policy. Discusses future implications of the policy.

20. BONDESTAM, Lars. "The Politics of Food on the Periphery." In *The Political Economy of Food*, pp. 215-264. Edited by
1978 Vilo Harle. Farnborough, Hants, England: Saxon House, Teakfield Ltd.

A discussion of the problems of food production, agricultural development, food aid and dependence from a socialist perspective. Shows how food policies of developed countries lead to under production and stagnation in third world countries. Focuses attention on the blockading of food production under precapitalism and the blockading of food distribution and consumption under capitalism.

21. BRANDOW, G.E. "Place of U.S. Food in Eliminating World Hunger." *American Academy of Political and Social Science*
1977 *Annals* 429: 1-11, January.

Includes policy suggestions for the provision of greater amounts of food aid than the modest amount now supplied on concessional terms by developed nations.

22. BROADBENT, K. "Agriculture, Environment and Current Policy in China." *Asian Survey* 16 (5): 411-26, May.
1976

Traces the evolution of China's agricultural and environmental problems and its relationship to education, economic and social development. Provides an alternative to U.S. food policy.

23. BROWN, Lester R. *The Politics and Responsibility of the North American Bread Basket.* Washington, D.C.: World-
1975 watch Institute. 43 p.

Presents basic facts about the dependence of developing nations on North American grain. Calls for a more explicit North American food policy (United States and Canada) to support a comprehensive global food strategy.

24. BROWN, Lester R. and ECKHOLM, Erik P. *By Bread Alone.* New York: Praeger Publishers. 272 p.
1974

Brief discussion of the decline of American food aid (from 1972 - 1974) in Chapter 5: Growing Global Food Insecurity. Indicates the current capacity of the international community to respond adequately to major food emergencies. Advocates a new international approach to food stockpiling and food aid. Concludes that food aid can be as valuable as any other resource transfer "when accompanied by appropriate recipient-government economic policies."

25.

1977

BROWN, Peter G. and SHUE, Henry, editors. <u>Food Policy: The Responsibility of the United States in the Life and Death Choices</u>. New York: The Free Press. 344 p.

A collection of eighteen original articles by nutritional analysts, political scientists, agricultural economists, ethical and social philosophers, farmer's representatives and government officials. Offers a wide range of analyses, opinions, and proposals on food export policy. Central to its theme is an examination of U.S. food policy with regard to world hunger. Topics discussed include: 1) poverty and food; 2) food as national property; 3) food aid, commercial exports, and the balance of payments; 4) the political uses of food aid; 5) a utilitarian framework for policy analysis in food-related foreign aid; 6) food aid and the free market; 7) a new legislative mandate for American food aid; 8) slowing population growth with food aid; 9) nutritional dilemmas of transforming economics; and 10) distributive criteria for development assistance.

26.

1971

BURKE, Melvin. "Does 'Food for Peace' Assistance Damage the Bolivian Economy?" <u>Inter-American Economic Affairs</u>. 25 (1): 3-19, Summer.

An examination of the impact of American food aid on the Bolivian economy. Contends that "Food for Peace" flour shipments to Bolivia "contributed to the rapid increase in domestic consumption, did nothing to increase the domestic production of wheat, and had an adverse effect upon the Bolivian milling industry leading to a decline in domestic flour production."

27.

1980

BUZZANELL, Peter J. "Brazil Outlines Strategy for Expanded Rice Output." <u>Foreign Agriculture</u>, 18: 12-13, July.

Outline of Brazil's four-point priority agricultural program to boost production, reduce dependence and eliminate the need for imports in drought years. The Country's major agricultural policies emphasize: 1) increasing yields in existing irrigated areas; 2) establishing new irrigation districts; 3) stimulating production of upland rice in areas of lower drought risk; and 4) generating new technology for upland rice in areas not favored by good distribution of rainfall.

28.   CALDWELL, Dan. <u>Food Crises and World Politics</u>. Beverly Hills: Sage Publications. 82 p.

1977

Two broad questions are addressed in this scholarly study: 1) How food policy decisions are made, and 2) What factors determine the effectiveness of relief of a food crisis. Discussion revolves around food policies during and after World Wars I and II. Includes a short analysis of the food crisis of 1972-74.

29.   CARBONELL, W. Jaffe and ROTHMAN, Harry. "An Implicit Food Policy: Wheat Consumption Changes in Venezuela." <u>Food Policy</u>, 2 (4): 305-317, November.

1977

Analysis of development policies and strategies acting as implicit food policies and aiding the progressive replacement of maize as the dietary staple by wheat.

30.   CHECCHI AND COMPANY. <u>Food for Peace, An Evaluation of P.L. 480 Title II: Volume One, A Global Assessment of Title II.</u> Washington, D.C.: Checchi and Company. 201 p.

1972

Appraisal and policy review of Title II P.L. 480 activity from 1954-1971 based on an eight-country sample. Reviews Title II programs in Ceylon, Colombia, the Dominican Republic, Ghana, Indonesia, Malaysia, Morocco, and the Phillipines. Discusses the origin and evolution of the Title II program and evaluates Title II impact in the areas of maternal child health, school feeding, food for work and supplemental cash support. Recommends that 1) increased emphasis be given to Title II as part of AID's package of development assistance; 2) Title II programming emphasize nutrition; 3) Title II priorities should emphasize maternal/child health and de-emphasize school feeding; 4) host governments assume greater responsibility for Title II planning; 5) multi-year country plans become the basis for Title II allocations; 6) more programming flexibility be allowed at the country level; and 7) voluntary agencies should be brought more closely into the planning process. Concludes that Title II makes a significant impact on the economic and human development of recipient countries.

31.   CHOU, Marylin, HARMON, David P. Jr., KAHN, Herman and WITTWER, Sylvan H. <u>World Food Prospects and Agricultural Potential</u>. New York: Praeger Publishers, 316 p.

1977

Chapter 7 provides an interesting summation of agricultural development problems of developing nations. Discusses institutional limitations to agricultural development, such as land tenure and reform, and the importance of a labor-intensive development strategy.

32.   CLAY, Edward. "Food Aid and Congressional Power," *Food Policy*, 4 (4): 305-6, November.

1979

Highlights of the January, 1979 seminar on Implementation of United States Food Aid -- Title III held at Princeton University. Describes congressional attempts to hedge the political use of food aid with legislative guidelines. Explains the mechanics and potential benefits of Title III P.L. 480 food aid, and suggests that "continued deference to the still dominant self-help ideology that baulks at giving something for nothing has flawed this legislation."

33.   CLAY, Edward J. "Food Aid and Food Policy in Bangladesh." *Food Policy*, 4 (2): 129-133, May.

1979

Bangladesh has replaced India as the largest recipient of food aid. The article attempts to fill a gap in the food aid literature and provides provisional evidence on the impact of food aid on the Bangladesh economy during the first quinquennium of 'planned' development, 1972/3 - 1977/8. Includes a discussion of foodgrain imports, P.L. 480, the World Food Program, food for work projects, disincentive effects on domestic agricultural production and the government's administration, distribution, and management of food aid programs.

34.   CLINE, William R., editor. *Policy Alternatives for a New International Economic Order*. New York: Praeger Publishers, Inc. 410 p.

1979

Using quantitative economic analysis, the contributing authors assess the impact of various proposals introduced in major international negotiating forums affecting the progress of less developed countries. A Chapter on "Grain Reserves, Emergency Relief, and Food Aid by Alexander H. Sarris, Philip C. Abbott and Lance Taylor discusses current problems from the Overseas Development Council's (ODC) frame of reference.

35.   COCHRANE, Willard W. *The World Food Problem: A Guardedly Optimistic View.* New York: Thomas Y. Crowell Company, Inc. 331 p.

1969

Defines and describes the world food problem in historical perspective; analyzes the problem in the context of the basic forces involved -- political, social, economic, technological, and demographic; and discusses policy actions required by both the developed and the developing countries to solve the problem permanently. Chapter 7 contains a lengthy discussion of foreign food aid including a historical description of: 1) the U.S. P.L. 480 Program from the early 1900's to 1968; 2) the magnitude of national and international food aid programs; and 3) the administrative problems of food aid. Describes specific descriptions of P.L. 480 aid and its impact on the countries of Israel, India, Tunisia and Latin America.

36.   COHN, Theodore H. *Canadian Food Aid: Domestic and Foreign Policy Implications.* Denver, Colorado: University of
1979 Denver, Graduate School of International Studies. 128 p.

Discusses Canada's food aid to the less developed countries, the procedure by which aid is given, the geographic distribution of aid, and the issue of "food power" -- i.e., the use of food aid for exerting political influence. Makes five major food aid policy proposals: 1) forward planning of food aid; 2) increased food aid through NGO's (non-governmental organizations); 3) increased multilateral food aid; 4) creation of global food reserves; and 5) increased technical assistance and research to food aid recipients.

37.   COUTSOUMARIS, G. *Analysis and Assessment of the Economic Effects of the United States P.L. 480 Programme in Greece.*
1965 Athens: Centre of Planning and Economic Research. 293 p.

An analysis of the impact of P.L. 480 on domestic food production in Italy. Particular emphasis is placed on domestic wheat cultivation. Concludes that: 1) P.L. 480 did not have any negative effects on domestic wheat production because wheat imports were small and support prices and other market regulations protected the small producer; 2) P.L. 480 maize imports bolstered livestock production; and 3) P.L. 480 seed oil imports contributed to increased consumption of oils among peasants.

38.   CROUCH, Luis and de JANVRY, Alain. "The Class Basis of Agricultural Growth." *Food Policy*, 5 (1): 3-13, February.
1980

Proposes that the development of agriculture in third world nations is uneven along class lines. Shows that 1) the dynamism of capitalist agriculture is often biased against wage-foods as a result of cheap food policies and directed instead toward the production of exportables, inputs for industry and luxury foods; and 2) the disappearance of peasants as a class of producers and their reduction to the role of labor reserve explains the crisis in many food crops and the reasons for rural poverty.

39. DANDEKAR, Vishnu Mahadeo. *Use of Food Surpluses for Economic Development, No. 33.* Poona, India: Gokhale Institute of Politics and Economics, 153 p.

1956

An early study of the potential development uses of food aid for nutritional, public works and labor intensive programs in India. Concludes that food surpluses can help finance total annual development expenditures.

40. DANTWALA, M.L. "Incentives and Disincentives in Indian Agriculture." *Indian Journal of Agricultural Economics.* 22 (2): 1-25.

1967

Analysis of the impact of P.L. 480 wheat imports on governmental price policies and the resulting incentives/disincentives to domestic production. Argues that P.L. 480 food imports did not significantly lower prices or alter growth rates.

41. DE MARCO, Susan and SECHLER, Susan. *The Fields Have Turned Brown: Four Essays on World Hunger.* Washington, D.C.: The Agribusiness Accountability Project. 139 p.

1975

The third essay in this collection, "The Food Aid Program" explains the political realities of American food aid. It concludes, "The United States knows far more about what works and what doesn't than we are currently using to make food aid policy, but until we begin using that knowledge to a constructive end for food aid recipients, the program will continue to be at best ineffectual, and at worst, injurious to the very peoples whose urgent needs are used as the justification for the program's existence." Other essays are: "The Importance of Grain," "The Green Revolution," and "Agribusiness Goes Abroad: Corporate Myths in a Hungry World."

42. DEPARTMENT OF STATE, Office of the Inspector General of Foreign Assistance. *Selected P.L. 480, Title II Programs in the Entente States of West Africa.* Washington, D.C.: Department of State, December. 14 p.

1976

An examination of the management of P.L. 480 programs in Benin, Ivory Coast, Niger, Togo and Upper Volta during 1962-1976.

43.   DEQUIN, Horst. *Agricultural Development in Malawi*. Munchen, Germany: IFO-Institut fur Wirtschafstorschung. 248 p.

1969

The first part describes the agricultural situation in Malawi including a discussion of the agricultural economy. The second part focuses on agricultural development policy from 1891-1968. Topics discussed include 1) guarantees for the rights of the European estates; 2) africanization in agricultural administration; and 3) the development concept according to the Policy of Discretionary Alignment or Non-Alignment.

44.   DIRKS, Harlan J. "Japan's Agricultural Policies Tied to Development of Imports." *Foreign Agriculture*. 12 (35): 2-5, 20, September.

1974

The first of a two-part series on Japan's agricultural policies. Topics discussed include Japan's determination to diversify import sources and gain new food supplies through increased overseas aid and investment; international food reserve policies; long-range policy goals for expanding and stabilizing total food supplies; and self-sufficiency in food production. Enumerates specific governmental policies.

45.   DIRKS, Harlan J. "Japan Ups Investment Overseas to Diversify Food Sources. *Foreign Agriculture*. 12 (36): 7-11,

1974   September.

Part II of a series on Japan's agricultural assistance programs. Claims that: "Japan's strategy for diversifying food import sources and gaining access to new food supplies is through greater investment of capital and through technical aid abroad." In upcoming years this aid is expected to emphasize overseas agricultural development programs.

46.   DODGE, Doris Jansen. *Agricultural Policy and Performance in Zambia: History, Prospects, and Proposals for Change*.

1977   Berkeley, California: Institute of International Studies, University of California, Berkeley. 285 p.

Reports Zambian food imports almost doubled between 1964 and 1973 and agricultural production has lagged. Highlights the conditions underlying Zambia's slow agricultural policy and performance in the pre-independence period. Shows that during this period the agricultural policies of the colonial administration favored European farming and discouraged agricultural production by African farmers. Chapter III shows how the agricultural policies of post-independence governments misdirected agricultural investment on capital intensive techniques only affecting a small number of farmers. Chapter IV examines crop pricing and marketing policy. Chapter VI presents an econometric estimation of the shadow price of traditional farm labor. Chapter VII presents the results of domestic resource cost calculations and Chapter VIII uses the findings to design a crop production policy for the Zambian government. Explains additional agricultural policies to increase production and to quicken the pace of agricultural development in Zambia.

47. DUDLEY, Leonard and SANDILANDS, Roger J. "The Side Effects of Foreign Aid: The Case of Public Law 480 Wheat in Colombia." Economic Development and Cultural Change. 23 (2): 325-336, January.

1975

A theoretical model for the marketing of surplus wheat imports. Shows that from 1958 to 1971, "the price received by Colombian producers averaged 20 percent lower than the estimated socially optimal level. As a result, Colombia imported 1,400,000 tons of wheat which could have been produced domestically at a lower opportunity cost." Concludes that the net gains to Colombia from P.L. 480 were probably positive; however, the "internal pricing policy, made difficult to resist by the terms of the agreements, cost the country the greater part of the potential benefits from the aid program."

48. DUNCAN, E. R., editor. Dimensions of World Food Problems. Ames, Iowa: Iowa State University Press. 309 p.

1977

A collection of articles discussing various dimensions of the role of food and agricultural production in development and stabilizing population. Chapter 14 explains food policies of governments; and Chapter 17 discusses assistance to developing nations.

49. ECONOMIC AND AGRICULTURAL DEVELOPMENT INSTITUTE AND MICHIGAN STATE UNIVERSITY. A Program of Research on Food for Peace: Part I, II and III. East Lansing, Michigan: Agency for International Development. 569 p.

1966

Outline of a program of research on "Food for Peace" sponsored by AID. Part I provides the purpose and use of the research map. It also summarizes major economic, financial, public policy, population, health, nutrition and social issues affecting the operation of "Food for Peace" in developing countries. Part II describes and prioritizes specific research projects which are presently underway or should be undertaken. Part III provides an annotated bibliography on "Food for Peace" from 1954-1966.

50.

1975

EHMAN, Frank W. "Swiss Agricultural Policy -- An Economic Juggling Act." <u>Foreign Agriculture</u>. 13 (24): 4, 14, June.

Explains that the agricultural policies of the Swiss Government are largely successful based on a delicate balance of centrally controlled policies on domestic production subsidies that boost internal food prices, and on international practices that restrict trade with other countries. Describes the mechanics of Swiss agricultural policies and their impact on U.S. markets.

51.

1980

EL-SHERBINI, Abdel Aziz. "Environmental Adversity and Food Policy in the Arab Gulf States." <u>Food Policy</u>. 5 (2): 97-104, May.

Suggests food policies for seven Gulf states: Iraq, Saudi Arabia, Kuwait, Bahrain, Qatar, Oman and the United Arab Emirates. Contends that harsh ecological conditions affecting agricultural production can be overcome with better management of complex enterprises and highly skilled manpower.

52.

1978

EL-SHERBINI, Aziz and SINHA, Radha. "Arab Agriculture: Prospects for Self-Sufficiency." <u>Food Policy</u>. 3 (2): 84-94, May.

Discusses the relative importance of the development of the agricultural sector despite oil revenues allowing massive food imports. Contends that food imports may be cut off by food-exporting countries for political reasons. Investigates the potential for Arab self-sufficiency and suggests several alternative strategies and food policies.

53.

1964

ESKILDSEN, C. R. "Aid -- The Beginning of Trade." <u>Foreign Agriculture</u>. 2 (2): 3-4, 15-16, January 13.

Historical review of P.L. 480's first decade of operation. Projects a 1980 food deficit of $25.6 billion in developing countries and a $25.3 billion surplus in developed countries, based on USDA statistical data. Calls for increased food aid as a method of expanding commercial markets.

54. FAMORIYO, Segun. "Food Production Policies in Nigeria," *Food Policy*. 3 (1): 50-58, February.

1978

Reviews Nigerian food production policies from 1919 to 1978. Describes the economic background to and the problems of Nigerian food production highlighting food processing and food marketing systems. Concludes that although projects like Operation-Feed-the-Nation and the National Accelerated Food Production Programme constitute immediate measures to halt reliance on food imports, the governmental approach to program implementation should be integrated with plans to modernize land tenure systems, adopt appropriate technologies and expand the country's infrastructure.

55. FIELD, John Osgood, and WALLERSTEIN, Mitchel B. "Beyond Humanitarianism: A Developmental Perspective on American Food Aid." In *Food Policy: The Responsibility of the Life and Death Choices*, pp. 234-258. Edited by Peter G. Brown and Henry Shue. New York: The Free Press.

1977

Describes the connecting links between food aid, malnutrition, and development. The thesis is "that food aid can make a meaningful contribution to development if it is targeted explicitly against protein-calorie malnutrition and if nutrition interventions utilizing food aid are, in turn, embedded in a multifaceted thrust against low productivity, high fertility, and pervasive poverty of rural populations." Makes a stimulating conceptual distinction between the developmental, political and humanitarian uses of food aid.

56. FIENUP, Darrell; BRANNON, Russell H.; and FENDER, Frank A. *The Agricultural Development of Argentina: A Policy and Development Perspective*. New York: Frederick A. Praeger, Publishers. 437 p.

1969

A study of changes in Argentinian agriculture up to 1966. Identifies the forces and factors responsible for agricultural production and defines the issues on which further research and policy decisions are needed. Chapter 8 focuses on the country's agricultural policy and discusses land, tenancy, labor, tax, marketing and pricing policies and agricultural credit in relation to their overall impact on agricultural policy.

57. FISHER, Franklin M. "A Theoretical Analysis of the Impact of Food Surplus Disposal on Agricultural Production in Recipient Countries." *Journal of Farm Economics*. 45 (4): 863-875, December.

1963

A theoretical analysis of the problems raised for the domestic agriculture of underdeveloped countries by the use of foreign food surpluses. The analysis is twofold: 1) How large and serious a discouragement to domestic agriculture is the importation of foreign food surpluses? 2) Given the type of expenditures for economic development to which the receipts for surplus sales are devoted, by how much do such expenditures offset any negative effect of the surplus by (directly or indirectly) encouraging development of domestic agriculture? Shows that price effects can be of considerable importance in policy evaluation and calls for econometric analysis of price effects on both supply and demand of agricultural commodities in underdeveloped countries.

58. FLETCHER, Lehman B., and MERRILL, William C., editors. <u>Latin American Agricultural Development and Policies.</u> Ames,
1968 Iowa: Department of Economics, Iowa State University. 90 p.

A collection of articles on agricultural development and policy in Argentina, Chile, Uruguay, Brazil, Colombia, Peru, Venezuela and Mexico.

59. FLOTO, Edgardo. "Chile: The Secular Food Crisis." <u>Food Policy</u>. 4 (2): 95-106, May.
1979

Examines the domestic food and agricultural polices of the Allesandri, Frei and Allende governments and concludes that "the highly concentrated land tenure system appears to be a decisive factor in explaining the crisis in Chilean agriculture."

60. FOOD AND AGRICULTURE ORGANIZATION OF THE UNITED NATIONS. <u>A Right to Food: A Selection from Speeches by Addeke H.</u>
1976 <u>Boerma, Director-General of FAO 1968-1975.</u> Rome: FAO. 177 p.

Chronicles FAO policies over this seven year period. Draws relationships between FAO policy, international economic and social development issues, international agricultural education, politics and nutrition. According to the Director-General, a "rapid advance of agriculture is needed in most developing countries....The very existence of the world food problem reflects the lag in agricultural output in many developing countries relative to the needs. To overcome this lag must be the immediate emphasis in development policy." The speeches "are grouped within certain themes, completed by a certain amount of background, connecting narrative and commentary necessary to an understanding of the issues involved."

61. FOOD AND AGRICULTURAL ORGANIZATION OF THE UNITED NATIONS. *A Strategy for Plenty: The Indicative World Plan for Agri-*
1970 *cultural Development.* Rome, Italy: FAO. 63 p.

Presents the main issues, conclusions and policy implications of the United Nations/FAO three-volume, 744 page Indicative World Plan (IWP) for Agricultural Development. The IWP is one of the FAO's most important contributions to the U.N. Second Development Decade. It contains a discussion of the major issues which will confront world agriculture in the 1970's and early 1980's and suggests food policies which could guide national and international actions to resolve the world food problem.

62. FOOD AND AGRICULTURAL ORGANIZATION OF THE UNITED NATIONS. *Agricultural Development in Nigeria 1965-1980.* Rome: FAO.
1966 512 p.

Presents various perspectives for agricultural development in Nigeria up to 1980. Parts A and B highlight policies and programs for the development and production of cocoa, rubber, oil-palm, ground-nuts, cotton, and other food and cash crops. Makes suggestions for the improvement of the internal organization of the ministry of Agriculture and Natural Resources.

63. FOOD AND AGRICULTURAL ORGANIZATION OF THE UNITED NATIONS. "Deadlock on Grain Reserves Prompts Five-Point Food
1979 Security Plan." *Ceres* 12 (3): 3-4, May - June.

A brief description of the 1979 failure of UNCTAD to establish a new International Grains Agreement and the weaknesses of the 1971 International Wheat Agreement. Discusses the content of the FAO's Five-Point Security Plan with regard to food reserves, food aid and the components of food security.

64. FOOD AND AGRICULTURE ORGANIZATION OF THE UNITED NATIONS. *Food Aid and Education,* World Food Program Studies, No. 6.
1965 Rome: FAO. 22 p.

Review of the role of education in the overall development process and the potential contribution of food aid. Analyzes the costs and benefits of providing various forms of food aid to primary school pupils, to students attending secondary schools, vocational training courses, and to persons participating in community development projects. Concludes that "Food aid used to further education is just as much a contribution to development as food aid in the traditional investment sectors."

65.

1964

FOOD AND AGRICULTURE ORGANIZATION OF THE UNITED NATIONS. Food Aid and Other Forms of Utilization of Agricultural Surpluses: A Review of Programs, Principles and Consultations. Rome, Italy: FAO. 55 p.

Investigates the raising of food consumption, agricultural and general economic development by the use of surpluses in the less developed countries. Chapters I - IV present a factual account of policies and programs relating to the utilization of U.S. agricultural surplus since 1954. Chapter V discusses major aspects of food aid programs and presents observations on the outlook for these programs.

66.

1970

FOOD AND AGRICULTURE ORGANIZATION OF THE UNITED NATIONS. Keys to Development. Rome, Italy: FAO.

Analyzes various food and development issues which affect food policy such as reduction of waste, closing the protein gap and the promotion of high-yielding cereal varieties.

67.

1965

FOOD AND AGRICULTURE ORGANIZATION OF THE UNITED NATIONS. Operational and Administrative Problems of Food Aid, by D. A. Fitzgerald. World Food Program Studies. No. 4. Rome: FAO. 63 p.

Proceeding on the assumption that the world's governments 1) favor a policy of food aid through complementary bilateral and multilateral programs; and 2) aim not only at surplus disposal but also at meeting user's needs, this study explores some of the principal operational and administrative problems of food aid. Topics discussed include donor and recipient food aid management problems; food aid negotiations; the relationship of food aid to long-range national development planning; participation of technical assistance missions in the preparation and execution of food-aided programs; the use of counterpart funds; and the relationship of food aid grants or sales to additional food consumption.

68.

1975

FOOD AND AGRICULTURE ORGANIZATION. Population, Food Supply and Agricultural Development. Rome: FAO. 62 p.

A study supervised by a Working Group of FAO's Economic and Social Policy Department. Provides the principal basis for FAO's contribution to the 1974 World Population and World Food Conferences. Discusses the relationships between population and food supply, the dimensions and causes of hunger and malnutrition, the demand for food and possibilities for increasing food production in Third World countries. Debates major international food policy questions. Concludes that "food aid will continue to be an essential element of world food security and international assistance for development. However, its effectiveness in yielding the desired results will be greatly enhanced if the concept of forward planning is agreed upon and if there is some assurance of continuity of food supplies at a minimum level, with the burden being shared between various countries on an equitable basis."

69.

1970

FOOD AND AGRICULTURE ORGANIZATION OF THE UNITED NATIONS. Provisional Indicative World Plan for Agricultural Development. Rome: FAO. 327 p.

An international frame of reference to help governments formulate and implement their agricultural and food policies. Synthesizes and updates important policy information on the Near East, South America, Africa South of the Sahara, Asia, and the Far East. The report suggests that agricultural policy should constantly adjust to food policy and discusses various aspects of this problem. (Chapter 13).

70.

1979

FOOD AND AGRICULTURE ORGANIZATION OF THE UNITED NATIONS. "Self-Sufficiency: Facts and Figures." Ceres 12 (1): 19-21, January-February.

Food self-sufficiency indicators are presented in graphic form. They show an upward trend in levels of food self-sufficiency in Asia, and the Far East, including the Asian centrally planned economies. "The most dramatic decline has been Africa where the self-sufficiency ratio has dropped from a high of 104 in 1963 to about 95 in 1975."

71.

1965

FOOD AND AGRICULTURE ORGANIZATION OF THE UNITED NATIONS. The Demand for Food, and Conditions Governing Food Aid During Development, by V. M. Dandekar. World Food Program Studies, No. 1. Rome: FAO. 69 p.

Discussion of the demand for food aid in terms of nutritional deficiencies, the gap between consumption and production of food, and the gap in the balance of payments of the developing countries. Considerations governing the use of food aid are 1) the availability of food supplies in the recipient country; 2) the prices, production, and marketed surplus of food grains; 3) the maintenance of existing development programs; 4) the use of the sales proceeds generated from food aid; 5) the additionality of food supplies; 6) the real costs and administration of works programs; and 7) the suitability of programs for financing through food aid. Contends that an independent autonomous statutory agency should administer the entire food aid program within a country to avoid the temptations of using food aid beyond its legitimate purpose.

72.

1965

FOOD AND AGRICULTURE ORGANIZATION OF THE UNITED NATIONS. The Impact of Food Aid on Donor and Other Food-Exporting Countries, by George R. Allen. World Food Program Studies, No. 2. Rome: FAO. 52 p.

Assesses food aid and agricultural policies in food-exporting countries and the indirect benefits or detrimental effects of food aid programs on third party commercial exporters. Discusses the social costs of producing food aid in terms of supply control and livestock production. Describes methods of securing the ideal product mix. Summarizes the effects of food aid on third party exporters in Israel, Colombia, Pakistan, India and Japan in Appendix 2. The general conclusion is that "while food surpluses have been an important means of aiding growth in developing countries, they are unlikely thereby to have induced a demand for commerical food imports as large as that which they displaced." Cautions that if "the practical alternative to the development of food aid programs was structural adaptation in the surplus producing countries and that consequence would not have been a substantial fall in prices in normal commercial markets, then third party exporters of wheat and coarse grains can claim that they have suffered economically from P.L. 480 and similar schemes."

73.

1965

FOOD AND AGRICULTURE ORGANIZATION OF THE UNITED NATIONS. The Linking of Food Aid with Other Aid, by S. Chakravarty and P. N. Rosenstein-Rodan. World Food Program Studies, No. 3. Rome: FAO. 39 p.

Discussion of general economic uses of food aid. The report makes an important distinction between commodity aid, particularly food aid, and nonspecific aid given in the form of loans or grants. Analytical relationships between these aid types are derived on the basis of conceptual issues. Distinctions are also made between the program and project approaches to food aid in developing countries. (See Chapter 2 and 3). Discusses food aid policy in Chapter 4. Chapter 5 and 6 focus on the co-ordination of food aid among aid-providing and aid-receiving nations. The main conclusion is that "food aid can best be used as a proportion of general aid for economic development, that is, within the framework of the total development program of a country."

74. FOOD AND AGRICULTURE ORGANIZATION OF THE UNITED NATIONS. *The Role of Multilateral Food Aid Programs*, by Jan Dessau. World Food Program Studies, No. 5. Rome: FAO. 38 p.

1965

Describes distinctive features and purposes of multilateral food aid programs which 1) provide yardsticks against which the role of multilateral food aid will be assessed; and 2) determine how and to what extent multilateral food aid might complement bilateral programs. Compares the respective advantages of multilateral and bilateral programs to work out an appropriate division of labor and organize satisfactory functional co-ordination. Reviews the past experience of multilateral programs and changing attitudes about food aid administration; and considers how maximum benefits from operating a multilateral program as a complement to bilateral arrangement can be secure.

75. FOOD AND AGRICULTURE ORGANIZATION. *The State of Food and Agriculture 1977*. Rome: FAO, 224 p.

1978

Annual report on world food and agriculture situation including an analysis of production, trade, demand, supply, farm and consumer prices. Special topics covered include factors affecting progress in food and agriculture in developing countries, and the state of natural resources and the human environment for food and agriculture.

76. FOWELS, H. A. "Eight Years of Agricultural Research Under P. L. 480." *Foreign Agriculture*. 4 (33): 5-6, August 15.

1966

Highlights achievements of agricultural research financed by foreign currencies earned from the sale of surplus agricultural commodities under Title I of P.L. 480.

77. FRAENKEL, Richard; HADWIGER, Don F.; and BROWNE, William P., editors. *The Role of U.S. Agriculture in Foreign Policy*. New York: Praeger Publishers. 253 p.

1979

An examination of the inter-connections between American agriculture and U.S. policy in foreign agricultural development. Focuses on the use of American agricultural exports as an instrument in the achievement of national objectives, and U.S. responsibility for world food security.

78.   FREEMAN, Orville L. "An Analysis: Goals and Results of Public Law 480." <u>Foreign Agriculture</u>. 6 (16): 2-4, April 15.
1968

Orville L. Freeman, then Secretary of Agriculture, compares results of Public Law 480 with its legislative objectives, commenting on both past benefits and 1968-69 aims, such as improving the U.S. balance-of-payments position and building U.S. agricultural markets.

79.   FREEMAN, Orville L. "What Public Law 480 Has Accomplished in 10 Years." <u>Foreign Agriculture</u>. 2 (21): 3-5, May 25.
1964

Orville L. Freeman, then Secretary of Agriculture provides his perspective on the accomplishments of the P.L. 480 program. He relates P.L. 480 benefits to U.S. incomes, expansion of commercial markets and humanitarian and foreign policy interests.

80.   FREUDENBERGER, C. Dean. and MINUS, Paul M. Jr. <u>Christian Responsibility in a Hungry World</u>. Nashville, Tennessee:
1976 Abingdon. 128 p.

Using "biblical wisdom and a sociological analysis of causes and possible solutions" of hunger, the authors propose guidelines for action.

81.   FREUND, Ron. "The Politics of Hunger: Food for Peace is Part of the American Arsenal." <u>Progressive</u>. 43 (12): 38-39,
1979 December.

Provides a brief historical summary of the political uses of the American food aid programs in developing countries.

82.   FRIEDMANN, Karen J. "Danish Agricultural Policy, 1870-1970: The Flowering and Decline of a Liberal Policy." <u>Food
1974 Research Institute Studies</u>. 13 (3): 225-238.

Describes Danish agricultural policy, 1870 to 1970, and identifies the conditions that made the liberal policy possible as well as those which caused this policy to be abandoned as support and subsidization measures were adopted.

83.   GEORGE, Susan. *Feeding the Few: Corporate Control of Food*.
      Washington, D.C.: Institute for Policy Studies.   79 p.
1978

   Discusses the New International Economic Order and what she
   calls the New Imperialist Economic Order. Focusses on agricultural development in underdeveloped countries and its
   place in the world food system. Discusses food policy and
   development choices of underdeveloped countries in relation
   to the role of United States agribusiness. Concludes that
   "food dependency conditions other kinds of dependency, and
   so long as a nation has failed to solve its own food problem, there is little chance that it can practice any truly
   independent policies, whether domestic or foreign."

84.   GEORGE, Susan.   *How the Other Half Dies: The Real Reasons
      for World Hunger*. New York: Allanheld, Osmun and Co. Pub-
1976 lishers. 308 p.

   Examination of the role of affluent nations "in keeping
   other people hungry." Chapter 8, "Food Aid?...Or Weapon?,"
   discusses the role of U.S. food aid from a power-politics
   standpoint. It documents the historical use of U.S. food
   aid to promote its own economic advantage and foreign-policy
   objectives. Describes the strings attached to American food
   aid and suggests that "in exchange for giving up their power
   of decision and a large degree of political and economic
   autonomy, food-aid-recipient nations cannot even be sure
   that the food will continue to arrive, at what time, or in
   what quantities."

85.   GHOSH, Rabindra Nath. *Agriculture in Economic Development
      with Special Reference to Punjab*. New Delhi: Vikas Pub-
1977 lishing House PVT LTD. 164 p.

   A systematic account of the remarkable growth of the Punjab
   region in India and a survey of the role of agriculture in
   economic development.

86.   GILBERT, Alvin E., and BIOLLEY, Vincent. "Morocco Seeks
      Sugar Self-Sufficiency by 1985." *Foreign Agriculture*. 14
1976 (21): 9-10, May 24.

   Description of Morocco's agricultural policies to reduce
   dependency on imported sugar.

87. GIRDNER, Janet; OLORUNSOLA, Victor; FRONING, Myrna; and HANSEN, Emmanuel. "Ghana's Agricultural Food Policy -- Operation Feed Yourself." Food Policy. 5 (1): 14-24, February.

1980

Article discusses the successes and shortcomings of "Operation Feed Yourself" -- a program instituted in 1972 by the Ghanaian military to bolster domestic agricultural production. It concludes that the potential of the program has been limited by poor management and encourages the Agricultural Development Bank to change its loan policies regarding small-scale food crop farmers.

88. GOERING, Theodore J. "Public Law 480 in Colombia." Journal of Farm Economics. 44 (4): 992-1004, November.

1962

An assessment of the impact of P.L. 480 upon Colombian agriculture between 1955 - 60. Areas of study include the price effect of P.L. 480 on the production of domestic cereals; the use of P.L. 480 local currency loans; and the impact of P.L. 480 on Colombia's trading pattern. Concludes that since the "Colombian environment includes a shortage of foreign exchange and lagging food production ... P.L. 480 met a need by permitting increased food imports at a time when balance of payments conditions dictated conservation in exchange expenditure."

89. GOLDICH, Judith G. "Changing Policies Shift USSR from Net Farm Exporter to Importer." Foreign Agriculture. 16 (49): 10-11, 13, December 4.

1978

A discussion of changing food policies in the USSR during the 1970's and its relationship to U.S. agricultural exports. Emphasizes the development and impact of consumer-oriented food policies in the USSR.

90. GREAT BRITAIN PARLIAMENT. House of Commons. Select Committee on Overseas Development. The World Food Crisis and Third World Development: Implications for U.K. Policy. London: HMSO. 370 p.

1976

Discusses types of aid to under-developed countries. Makes recommendations to continue and improve British support of food and rural development projects in Third World Countries.

91. GREEN, Daniel. The Politics of Food. London: Gordon Cremonesi. 220 p.

1975

Examines factors which affect governmental food policies including pressure groups, ideology, history, etc.

92. GREENSHIELDS, Bruce L. "Japan Launches Three-Pronged Agricultural Policy Program." <u>Foreign Agriculture</u>. 12 (1): 2-
1974   4, January 7.

A description of Japan's programs to increase agricultural self-sufficiency, to expand stocks of grains and oilseeds, and to accelerate the diversification of supply sources. The new plan was initiated as a result of supply and price instability in world markets.

93. GREENSTON, P. M. <u>The Food for Peace Program and Brazil: Valuation Effects of Commodity Inflow.</u> (Dissertation)
1972   Minneapolis, Minnesota: University of Minnesota, USA. 159 p.

Measures 1) the aid component of the P.L. 480 flow of wheat to Brazil; 2) the impact of P.L. 480 on domestic producer and consumer prices; and 3) the relationship between food imports and the quantity of food produce.

94. GRIFFIN, Philip. "The Impact of Food Aid -- Peru, a Case Study." <u>Food Policy</u>. 4 (1): 46-52, February.
1979

After visiting Peru as a member of the OECD Development Centre team, the author describes the impact of food aid on the country. He discusses food aid planning, food for work projects administration, management and the governmental responsibilities of donors and recipients. The author concludes that project aid has more advantages than programme aid; and that in the case of Peru food aid showed additional consumption and contributed to economic development.

95. GUSTAFSSON, Mervi. "The Development of International Food Aid." In <u>The Political Economy of Food</u>. pp. 94-129. Edited
1978   by Vilo Harle. Farnborough, Hants, England: Saxon House, Teakfield Ltd.

An historical analysis of the food aid programs and policies of the United States, the EEC, the Soviet Union and the Nordic Countries. Includes brief description of the food aid research undertaken by the Food Study Group of the International Peace Research Association at the University of Tampere, Finland.

96. GWATKIN, Davidson R. "Food Policy, Nutrition Planning and Survival." Food Policy 4 (4): 245-258, November.

1979

   Presents data suggesting that the food and nutrition policies of Sri Lanka and Kerala contribute to rapid health improvements and remarkable social and economic achievements. Discusses small farmer agricultural development, public food distribution, nutritional status, per capita food availability and the composition of the diet. Two major conclusions are: 1) "low mortality rates can coexist not only with low incomes but also with low overall food supplies, when the types of food available are varied enough to provide a well-balanced diet and distributed equitably; and 2) if governmental food policies are deeply concerned about the political support and well-being of the poor majority, the effectiveness of food and nutrition programs will be enhanced.

97. HADWIGER, Don F., and BROWNE, William P., editors. The New Politics of Food. Farnborough, Hants, UK: Lexington Books, Teakfield Ltd. 267 p.

1979

   An extensive review of agricultural policy in American political institutions. Discusses domestic food policy issues such as food stamps and environmental protection.

98. HALCROW, Harold. Food Policy for America. New York: McGraw-Hill. 264 p.

1977

   An examination of United States agricultural and food policy including a review of nutritional and health objectives; and agricultural structures and price policies which may lead to improvement of production and consumption levels. A basic textbook approach is used to present a detailed discussion of the historical development of present U.S. policies and concepts within the grasp of the non-specialist.

99. HALL, Lana L. "Evaluating the Effects of P.L. 480 Wheat Imports on Brazil's Grain Sector." American Journal of Agricultural Economics 62 (1): 19-28, February.

1980

   Analysis of the positive impact of P.L. 480 wheat imports on grain production in Brazil based on the findings of an econometric analysis of the country's grain sector. "The results also show that P.L. 480 imports, in spite of the Usual Marketing Requirements (UMR) imposed, . . . [a] disruption of international commercial wheat markets which has obvious implication for third-country wheat exporters."

100. HALL, Lana L. "Food Aid and Agricultural Development: The Case of P.L. 480 Wheat in Latin America." (Research Essay, Typewritten Report) Berkeley, California: University of California, Berkeley. 50 p.

1977

Develops a framework of analysis to determine whether U.S. food aid (particularly U.S. wheat imports) have contributed to growth or stagnation of the agricultural sectors of developing nations. Focuses on the production, consumption and trade of cereals and feedgrains in Brazil, Colombia and Peru from 1955-75. Analyzes the possibility of the P.L. 480 imports having increased dependence on wheat imports from the U.S. and whether this dependence has been beneficial or detrimental. The effects of U.S. wheat imports on the intra-regional wheat trade of the Latin American Free Trade Association (LAFTA) are also analyzed. Chapter Three describes government policy variables affecting the production, consumption and trade of grain focusing on price support systems, tariff and import restrictions and exchange rates.

101. HALLOWELL, Elmer W. "Italy Strives to Boost Food Self-Sufficiency, Emphasis Put on Meat." *Foreign Agriculture* 16 (7): 10-11, February 13.

1978

"To boost Italy's overall food self-sufficiency ratio to about 90 percent and thereby to reduce the balance-of-payments deficit for food, Minister of Agriculture Giovanni Marcora has proposed the investment of about 9 billion lire in expanded agricultural production over a 5-year period ending in 1981." The author describes the details of this policy.

102. HARLE, Vilho, editor. *The Political Economy of Food.* Farnborough, Hants, England: Saxon House, Teakfield Ltd. 438 p.

1978

A team from the International Food Politics Research Group at the University of Tampere analyze the food crisis in the context of the world economic structure. The essays examine the relationships between food imports and neo-colonialism; international food production and trade; international agribusiness; international food aid; food as a political weapon; dependence and self-reliance; and agricultural development and its international and social implications. This book provides illuminating insights into the establishment and workings of national and international food policies.

103.   HATHAWAY, Dale E. "Farm Policies Vital to Farmer, Consumer, and Foreign Customer." <u>Foreign Agriculture</u> 15 (34): 2-3,
1977   August 22.

    Excerpts from a speech of Dale E. Hathaway, then U.S. Assistant Secretary of Agriculture for International Affairs and Commodity Programs before the National Association of Farm Broadcasters. Briefly reviews problems of U.S. food and agriculture policies. Suggests that "what we need are actions that essentially will provide a cushion of adequate supplies, insuring our own food security while protecting consumers abroad who depend on U.S. agriculture for supplies. This must be done within a framework that assures fair returns for the U.S. producer. These goals are not inconsistent."

104.   HATHAWAY, Dale E. "Status of International Grain Agreements." <u>Foreign Agriculture</u> 12 (15): 6-7, June.
1979

    A discussion of the 1971 International Wheat Agreement including a Wheat Trade Convention and a Food Aid Convention. Provides the U.S. perspective on three pivotal issues, the size of reserve stock commitments, price levels for reserve stock accumulation and release, and special provisions for developing countries. Describes U.S. attempts to establish a special Food Security Reserve, which has been called the International Emergency Wheat Reserve.

105.   HATTI, Neelambar. "Impact of Assistance Under PL 480 on Indian Economy 1956-1970." <u>Economy and History</u> 20 (1):
1977   23-40.

    Investigates the impact of P.L. 480 imports focusing on investment, and consumption, balance-of-payments prices and production of food grains, in particular wheat. An examination of the share of P.L. 480 funds in the resources of the second and third five-year plans and annual plans. Shows that P. L. 480 provided them with significant financial resources. However, the inflationary impact of the second five-year plan was largely neutralized by P.L. 480 imports. According to the author, "The resources, which in the absence of the imports under P.L. 480 would probably have been diverted to agricultural industries producing such inputs as fertilisers, insecticides were allocated to the development of heavy and basic industries with long gestation periods. This diversion of resources probably created structural and market imbalances, with adverse effects felt subsequently." Pointing to the political uses of P.L. 480 and the American share of counterpart funds, the author concludes that "despite some beneficial aspects of P.L. 480 imports for India, it cannot be overlooked that the programme undermined India's determination to tackle the agricultural problems and was largely responsible for the lack of a vigorous agricultural policy in India until the mid-sixties."

106. HEDLEY, Douglas, and PEACOCK, David. Food for Peace, P.L. 480 and American Agriculture: Agricultural Economic Report No. 156. East Lansing, Michigan: Michigan State University. 36 p.

1970

Provides an historical review of U.S. agricultural export policies from 1865 to 1965. Shows that the provisions of P.L. 480 are not entirely new. The largest importers of Titles I and IV of P.L. 480 from 1955 through 1969 are enumerated. The final part of this report deals with "the influence of P.L. 480 upon the economies of the nations involved: 1) the U.S., 2) the nations selling the same agricultural products as the U.S. exports under P.L. 480, and 3) the nations receiving commodities under P.L. 480."

107. HEYER, Judith; MAITHA, J. K.; SENGA, W. M., editors. Agricultural Development in Kenya: An Economic Assessment. Nairobi: Oxford University Press. 372 p.

1976

A systematic account of the country's agricultural development from the colonial era to the post-independent periods of the 1960's and early 1970's. An overview of Kenyan agricultural development policy is provided in Chapter 4. Points out the relationships between agricultural development and economic planning.

108. HOPKINS, Raymond F; PUCHALA, Donald J.; and TALBOT, Ross B., editors. Food, Politics and Agricultural Development: Case Studies in the Public Policy of Rural Modernization. Boulder, Colorado: Westview Press. 311 p.

1979

A collection of nine articles emphasizing the politics of agricultural development and agricultural policy in both developed and developing countries. The politics behind the agricultural policies of England, France, Denmark, the Soviet Union, China, Pakistan, South Korea, Iran and various countries in Africa are given special attention.

109. HOWARD, James O. "Low-Priced Food Policy Works in South Africa." Foreign Agriculture 16 (47): 7-9, November 20.

1978

A brief discussion of the components of South Africa's low-priced food policy including: 1) agricultural import policy and goals of self-sufficiency; 2) low production costs; 3) food processing costs; 4) farm income support program; 5) single channel fixed price schemes; 6) floor price and surplus removal schemes; and 7) supervisory controls.

110. HSU, King-Yi. <u>Political Mobilization and Economic Extraction: Chinese Communist Agrarian Policies during the Kiangsi Period.</u> New York: Garland Publishing, Inc. 365 p.

1980

A review of the food and agricultural policies of the Chinese Soviet Republic established by the Chinese Communists in Jui-chin, Kiangsi in November, 1931, and continued until October 1934. These policies were the foundation of modern Chinese agricultural policies.

111. HUGHES, T. Walter. "U.S. Donates 26 Billion Pounds of Food Overseas in 17 Years." <u>Foreign Agriculture</u> 5 (13): 9-10, March 27.

1967

A review of the accomplishments of U.S. food aid programs from 1950 to 1967. Food aid legislation from 1949 to 1967 is highlighted.

112. HUNGATE, Lois Simonds, and SHERMAN, Ralph W. <u>Food and Economics.</u> Westport, Connecticut: AVI Publishing Company, Inc. 244 p.

1979

On the premise that "demand for food competes with demand for other economic goods and that these demands must be met largely within each nation, not from international trade or from gifts from wealthier nations," the authors contend that "It does little good to attempt to introduce better food production technology into a shortage nation if prospective consumers cannot buy the food produced." Furthermore, the rate of economic development may be limited by population growth. Food aid in the future will probably become less available, therefore underdeveloped nations are encouraged to depend on producing their own food. The latter is especially important since: "International trade in food will continue to account for less than 10% of the world's food." The authors predict that the year 2000 will not see the food problem solved. Also discusses issues of food and international trade, world food production potentials and food and development. Chapter 11, National Food Policies, includes a comprehensive treatment of the factors affecting the formulation and implementation of food policy including economic principles, farm income, food prices, subsidies and government control.

113. HUTCHINS, James A. Jr. "Food for Peace Moves Toward Dollar Terms." *Foreign Agriculture* 8 (32): 2-4, August 10.

1970

Reviews progress toward the goal of P.L. 480 dollar financing. "The rapid transition to dollar sales . . . saw a drop in value of commodities exported under sales agreements, a substantial rise in the value of new sales agreements entered into, and a slight gain in the value of commodities that were donated to foreign countries." Highlights food aid composition, balance-of-payments benefits, self-help activities and foreign currency uses of P.L. 480 in 1969.

114. INSTITUTE FOR FOOD AND DEVELOPMENT POLICY. *The Aid Debate: Assessing the Impact of U.S. Foreign Assistance and the World Bank*. San Francisco, California: Institute for Food and Development Policy. 82 p.

1979

Deals with the consequences of American food aid in developing countries. Highlights the impact of food aid on market development, agricultural production and the agricultural development policies of various food aid recipients. Describes the use of food aid as a political weapon and a guise for military aid. Contends that "the overriding impact of the United States on the ability of people to become food self-reliant is not through food aid but through the corporate, military, economic and covert involvement of the United States in their countries."

115. INTERNATIONAL FOOD POLICY RESEARCH INSTITUTE. *Food Needs of Developing Countries: Projections of Production and Consumption to 1990*. Washington, D.C.: International Food Policy Research Institute. 157 p.

1977

Based on the assumption that production will grow in the next 15 years at the average annual rates of 1960-75, the low income countries of Asia and Sub-Sahara Africa will face severe food production deficits in 1990. Gives specific food production and consumption trends for most developing nations. Describes food policy alternatives. Indicates that food aid and food imports will have to increase "well in excess of recent levels . . . to prevent further deterioration of already inadequate diets."

116. INTERNATIONAL FOOD POLICY RESEARCH INSTITUTE. *Recent and Prospective Developments in Food Consumption: Some Policy Issues*. Washington, D.C.: International Food Policy Research Institute. 61 p.

1977

"Provides additional dimensions to the food problem, estimates of the numbers of people who are underfed and the amount of foodgrains that would be needed to provide them with the required energy (calorie) standard. Discusses basic policy issues at the national and international levels which would need to be resolved if there is to be progress in alleviating hunger and malnutrition."

117. ISENMAN, Paul J., and SINGER, H. W. "Food Aid: Disincentive Effects and Their Policy Implications." Economic Development and Cultural Change, 25 (2): 205-237, January.

1977

A review of the analytical issues and literature about the disincentive effects and risks of food aid. Deals with food aid (largely foodgrains) for development purposes. Suggests "that in food-short countries a sizable proportion of total development aid can often be in the form of food aid without a significant cost in the efficiency of aid or in incentives for domestic agriculture. Food aid will not have a significant disincentive effect on the overall agricultural policies of the recipient government, "if a country has a strong commitment to agriculture and the political will and sound policies to carry out that commitment . . ." The appendix includes specific information on the price effect of food aid on foodgrain output in India.

118. ISENMAN, Paul, and SINGER, H. W. "The Price-Disincentive Effect of Food Aid Revisited: A Reply." Economic Development and Cultural Change, 27 (3): 553-554, April.

1979

A response to the critique of Peter Svedberg concluding that "The extent to which food aid results in additional food imports must be analyzed on a case-by-case basis. The continued existence of commerical food imports per se is not an indication that the same level of food imports would have taken place without the food aid."

119. ISHIKAWA, Shigeru. Agricultural Development Strategies in Asia: Case Studies of the Philippines and Thailand. Tokyo, Japan: The Asian Development Bank. 128 p.

1970

An empirical study of agricultural development problems of Thailand and the Philippines. Examines the bottlenecks and impediments that prevent or delay the pace of agricultural development. Derives agricultural development policy recommendations for Asia.

120. IVERSON, S. C.; IVERSON, K. L.; and KEVANY, J. P. "Food and Nutrition Policy Formulation--a Delphi Approach to Establishing Basic Principles." <u>Food Policy</u> 4 (1): 26-34, February.

1979

Results of a multidisciplinary, international Delphi inquiry to establish basic principles for food and nutrition policy formulation. Sets up preliminary assumptions, establishes a working food and nutrition policy vocabulary and defines controversial topics. Results in consensus on several policy statements which provides a basis for the establishment of guidelines in the development of flexible food and nutrition programs.

121. JOHNSON, D. Gale. <u>World Food Problems and Prospects</u>, Washington, D.C.: American Enterprise Institute for Public Policy Research. 83 p.

1975

A discussion of the myriad causes and consequences of world hunger. Chapters 6 and 7 focus on the problems of 1) grain reserves and price stability; and 2) increasing food production in developing countries.

122. JONES, David. <u>Food and Interdependence--The Effect of Food and Agricultural Policies of Developed Countries on the Food Problems of Developing Countries</u>. London: ODI. 52 p.

1976

The study pays particular attention to the policies of the United Kingdom and its partners in the Common Market (EEC).

123. JONES, David. "Food Interdependence and Europe." <u>ODI Review</u> (2): 25-37.

1975

Examination of problems which may be affected by food and agricultural policies of the European Community including: 1) the race between world food production and consumption; 2) the growing dependence of LDCS on DCS food production; 3) implications for developed country policy; 4) security stocks and EEC production; and 5) EEC food aid availability.

124. JONES, David B., and TULLOCH, Peter. "Is Food Aid Good Aid?" <u>ODI Review</u>: (2): 1-6.

1974

Discussion of the pros and cons of food aid and conditions for its most effective use. Concludes that "food aid--without measures to raise local incomes--is an inadequate response to the needs of food-deficit developing countries." Adds that "Food aid is bad aid: by lowering prices, and providing cheap food, it reduces the incentive to increase food production in recipient countries; similary, it allows recipient governments to neglect long-term supply problems."

125. JONSSON, U. "Towards a Food and Nutrition Policy in Tanzania." Food Policy 5 (2): 143-147, May.

1980

Historical survey of the colonial and post independence development of food and nutrition policies in Tanzania.

126. JOSLING, T. E. "Agricultural Policies in Developed Countries: A Review." Journal of Agricultural Economics 25 (3): 229-263, September.

1974

A survey and evaluation of recent contributions by economists to the analysis of agricultural policies in developed countries. Examines the interaction among general economic and specifically agricultural policies and reveals a number of areas where more research is needed.

127. JOSLING, Tim. "The European Community Agricultural Policies and the Interest of Developing Countries." ODI Review (1): 11-23. London: Overseas Development Institute.

1979

Describes the impact of the European Community, particulary the Common Agricultural Policy (CAP), on Third World Countries based on the interaction between developed country farm policies and developing country interests in the distributional implications of world price changes.

128. JOSLING, Timothy. Developed-Country Agricultural Policies and Developing-Country Suppliers: The Case of Wheat. Washington, D.C.: International Food Policy Research Institute. 67 p.

1980

Briefly discusses the role of food aid discussed in the empirical sections of the report describing the interdependence of food policies in the world food system. Examines the wheat sectors of Australia, Canada, the European Community, Japan, and the United Kingdom, and the United States from 1969/70 to 1977/78 to determine to what extent and how wheat availability in developing countries is destabilized by developed-country policies. Suggests that "these destabilizing forces are substantial and underscore the need for countervailing policies at the national and international levels."

129. KANEDA, Hiromitsu. "Structural Change and Policy Response in Japanese Agriculture after the Land Reform." *Economic Development and Cultural Change* 28 (3): 469-486, April.

1980

An assessment of the impact of land reform in Japan tracing the sources and rates of productivity growth in Japanese agriculture over some 30 years since the initiation of the land reform. Reviews the changing emphasis in agricultural price policy.

130. KERN, Clifford R. "Looking a Gift Horse in the Mouth: The Economics of Food Aid Programmes." *Political Science Quarterly* 83 (1): 59-75, March

1968

Supports the use of food aid to build up food reserves. Argues that negative policy and price effects of food aid can be overcome if the recipient country employs "measures which minimize harmful price effects."

131. KHAN, Kabir-ur-Rahman, "International Cocoa Agreement. 1975." *Food Policy* 4 (1): 15-25, February.

1979

Provides analysis of the regulation of the world cocoa market by the International Cocoa Agreement 1975 from a legal perspective. Examines its value as a tool for achieving the goals of the New International Economic Order.

132. KAHN, Kabir-ur-Rahman, "International Coffee Agreement 1976: Issues of Selectivity, Regulation and Reciprocity." *Food Policy* 3 (3): 180-190, August.

1976

A substantive discussion of the main provisions of the International Coffee Agreement 1976 (ICA). Points out the problems and peculiarities of this international commodity agreement and demonstrates how, unlike most other commodity agreements, the ICA 1976 serves primarily to regulate conflicts among producers rather than between importing and exporting nations.

133. KAHN, Kabir-ur-Rahman, "The International Sugar Agreement 1977: Market Regulator and Instrument of International Policy." *Food Policy* 3 (2): 104-112, May.

1978

Examination of the 1977 International Sugar Agreement in its context as an instrument of international food policy. Defines the rights and duties of importing and exporting countries under this commodity agreement and its relation to the New International Economic Order.

134. KLAASSE BOS, Andries. "Food Aid by the European Communities: Policy and Practice." <u>ODI Review</u> No. 1: 38-52.
1978

Describes the food aid program of the European Communities on the basis of three policy issues: 1) the criteria used to select recipients; 2) the relative merits of direct and indirect utilization; and 3) the value of counterpart funds. Encourages the EEC to increase its share of food aid, to relax its administrative procedures, to distribute more food aid to vulnerable groups and to drop its conditional approval of the use of counterpart funds.

135. KOFI, Tetteh A. "On Understanding Food-Aid and Agricultural Crises in the Third World, 1954-1975." <u>The Catalyst: Publication of the Stanford Forum</u>, 2 (1): 22-28, Autumn.
1975

Shows how food aid perpetuates underdevelopment in the Third World and discusses various national and international food aid programs which contribute to dependency. "It could be argued that food aid has affected the economic foundation--the base, and also the ideological forms, the superstructure--and perhaps has unduly postponed the era of social reform or revolution. In the meantime, food aid has fostered Third World dependency on high-cost United States loans and grants. In addition, food imports have exceeded demand and have held back agricultural production."

136. KRIESBERG, Martin. "IFAD--New UN Agency--Joins Effort to End World Food Shortage." <u>Foreign Agriculture</u> 16 (8): 14-15, February, 20.
1978

A discussion of the administrative and operational mechanics of IFAD--the International Fund for Agricultural Development--proposed at the 1974 world food conference. The agency provides food aid and agricultural development assistance to developing countries and may establish a precedent and a formula for development financing by OPEC governments.

137. KUO-CHUN, Chao. <u>Agrarian Policy of the Chinese Communist Party 1921-1959.</u> Westport, Connecticut: Greenwood Press, Publishers. 399 p.
1977

"This study represents an effort to describe and analyse: (1) the background of the agrarian problem in China; (2) the genesis of the agrarian policy of the Chinese Communist Party (CCP) since its foundation in 1921; (3) the major contents and results of the recent (1953-1959) agrarian programmes in China; (4) the characteristics and significance of these programmes; and (5) the problems as well as prospects of the CCP agrarian reform."

138.   LAPPE, Frances Moore, and COLLINS, Joseph. <u>Food First:</u>
       <u>Beyond the Myth of Scarcity</u>. Boston: Houghton Mifflin Co.
1977   466 p.

An innovative analysis of the world food situation based on the achievement of food security for each developing nation. "The heaviest constraint on food production and distribution turns out to be the inequality generated by our type of economic system--the system now being exported to the under-developed countries as the supposed answer to their food problems." Therefore, "more important than food aid or designing some rural development project for the Third World is building a movement in this country (United States) that makes the connection between the way government, corporate, and landed elites continue to undermine food security both here and abroad." Part 9, "The Helping Handout: Aid for Whom?" resolves that 1) the United States can never be a source of food security; 2) food aid reserves must be controlled by a multilateral institution in order to lessen the opportunity for political and commercial manipulation; 3) food aid should be used to create the preconditions for food self-reliance; and 4) concerned Americans should focus attention on the process of how hunger is created." Includes extensive reference and bibliographical notes.

139.   LAPPE, Frances Moore, and COLLINS, Joseph. <u>World Hunger:</u>
       <u>Ten Myths</u>. San Francisco, California: Institute for Food
1978   and Development Policy. 54 p.

Basic treatise on the root causes of world hunger. "Makes connections between the way the U.S. government and agribusiness oligopolies work against the hungry abroad and the way they work against the food interests of the vast majority of people in our own country." The authors contend that "food redistribution programs like food aid will, therefore never solve the problem of hunger" unless food aid is "given to those countries where the rural population is in the process of taking control over food-producing resources." Emphasis is placed on food self-sufficiency and agricultural development as a way for people to produce the food they need and secondarily, to generate foreign exchange.

140. LEGG, W. J., and SZCZEPANIK, E. F. "EEC Food Policies for the 1990's." <u>Futures</u> 10: 342-3, August.

1978

A short, provacative comparison of European food policies and their implications for the future.

141. LELE, Uma, and AGARWAL, Mohan. "Foodgrain Imports: Whether, When and How?" <u>Ceres</u> 12 (6): 20-25, November-December.

1979

Discussion of the relationship between foodgrain imports and food price policies in developing countries. The authors suggest that adroitly managed imports can benefit both consumer welfare and producer incentives.

142. LEVI, John. <u>African Agriculture: Economic Action and Reaction in Sierra Leone.</u> Oxford: Commonwealth Bureau of

1976 Agricultural Economics. 428 p.

Analyzes governmental agricultural development policies in relation to the economics of the Sierra Leonian agricultural sector as a whole. Chapter 8 makes agricultural policy recommendations and describes various development projects.

143. LEVI, John. "African Agriculture Misunderstood: Policy in Sierra Leone." <u>Food Research Institute Studies</u> 13 (3):

1974 239-262.

Analysis of the impact of agricultural policies on the economic mechanism of agriculture in Sierra Leone. Emphasis is placed on policy towards agricultural exports, particularly the production of rice, the staple food.

144. LIBBIN, Susan A. "U.S. Food-Aid Share Dips, But Is Still No. 1." <u>Foreign Agriculture</u> 15 (43): 9-11, October, 24.

1977

U. S. food aid--mainly agricultural commodities shipped under P. L. 480 and the Food for Peace Act--remained fairly constant in value until recently. The U. S. share of food aid has declined as other developed nations, notably Canada, Japan, and the European Community have increased their share, which stood at 41 percent in 1975, compared with less than 10 percent during 1960-68. Shows that as the sale of U. S. commercial farm exports rises, the P. L. 480 share of total U. S. agricultural exports declines.

145. LIPTON, Michael. "Urban Bias and Food Policy in Poor Countries." <u>Food Policy</u> 1 (1): 41-52, November.

1975

Contends that urban bias has led to inadequate, ill-directed and maldistributed farm inputs, poor agricultural planning, and growth with hunger. Describes three types of food policies affecting: 1) food availability; 2) inputs into food production; and 3) the conversion efficiency of farm inputs for better nutrition. Effective food policies should include: 1) raising the share of the national effort in improving the distribution and structure for food production; 2) retiming, restructuring and relocating calorie consumption; and 3) altering priorities in research and trade.

146. LU, C. C. <u>The Role of Food Aid, Agricultural Development and Capital Formation in Economic Development: A Case Study of Taiwan</u>. Dissertation. Ames, Iowa: Iowa State University. 317 p.

1973

An analysis of the growth of Taiwan's agricultural output and productivity using Harrod-Domar, Slow and Keynesian growth models. Study delineates the positive and negative effects of P. L. 480 food aid on Taiwan's economic growth. It concludes that Taiwan's economic development depends on the country's agricultural development.

147. MACKENZIE, Colin. "Self-sufficiency: An Interview with John Malecela of Tanzania." <u>Ceres</u> 12 (1): 22-28, January-February.

1979

Describes the details and implications of the FAO Regional Food Plan for Africa in the context of 1) building Africa's food production; 2) agricultural investment; 3) storage and post-harvest losses; and 4) inter-African food trade.

148. MANN, Jitendar S. "The Impact of Public Law 480 Imports on Prices and Domestic Supply of Cereals in India: Reply." <u>American Journal of Agricultural Economics</u>, 50 (1): 145-47, February.

1968

"The net contribution of P. L. 480 imports to consumption is always positive," and "the efficacy of the fair price shops in maintaining the price level of cereals is worth investigating; but the sketchy surmises which have been thrown around are not at all conclusive." According to Mann, "An imaginative price policy combined with measures to increase fertilizer production, improve soil and water management, provide agricultural credit, and control floods can bring about the desired increase in the domestic supply of food in India and eliminate the need for P. L. 480 imports in the long run."

149. MANN, Jitendar S. "The Impact of Public Law 480 Imports on Prices and Domestic Supply of Cereals in India." Journal of Farm Economics 49 (1): 131-145, February.

Analysis of the impact of cereals under Public Law 480 on prices and domestic cereals supply on the basis of an econometric model encompassing six simultaneous equations. The statistical analysis shows that P. L. 480 imports may lead to lower prices and a decline in domestic supply but that the decrease in domestic supply is less than the quantity imported. Thus, "there is a net addition to the quantity available for consumption, which is a significant contribution to a shortage economy."

150. MARX, Herbert L., Jr., Editor. The World Food Crisis. New York: The H. W. Wilson Co., 1975. 213 p.

1975

Each collected article discusses one of the following aspects of the world food problem from different points of view: 1) particular famine crisis areas; 2) the interrelation between food supply and population growth; 3) plans and achievements to increase food supply in developing nations; and 4) perspective food aid and food policy roles of the United States and various international agencies in the future.

151. MASON, Edward M. "Economic Development in India and Pakistan." Occasional Papers in International Affairs 13.

1966 Cambridge, Massachusetts: Harvard University. 67 p.

Includes an examination of the impact of P. L. 480 food aid policy on agricultural production. "There is evidence both in India and Pakistan that the ready availability of P. L. 480 food shipments postponed serious attention to the question of agricultural productivity. During the First Plan period in Pakistan (1955-60) it was argued, both inside and outside the Planning Commission, that, considering the availability of P. L. 480, it would be a waste of scarce material and human resources to give a higher priority to agriculture." The author also discusses the choice between the adoption of difficult measures to increase domestic food production and the easy reliance on food aid. He contends that the latter policy issue makes it difficult to assign a "development" value to food aid.

152.   MAXWELL, Simon. "Direct Versus Indirect Support of Public Works with Food Aid." In *Food Aid for Development*, pp. 103-116. Edited by Hartmut Schneider. Paris: Development Centre of the OECD.

1978

Pointing out the relationships between food aid, food for work and public works, the author challenges food for work critics. He makes a case for the use of food aid for public works programs and investigates the feasibility of the following contentions: 1) food-for-work provides a general macroeconomic advantage by eliminating or at least reducing the demand for other commodities, insulating the project economically from the rest of the economy, and preventing any disincentive effect on local agriculture; 2) payment in food acts as an incentive to local participation on projects which then become quasi-voluntary; 3) payment in food might have a favorable nutritional impact by increasing the proportion of income devoted to nutritious food; and 4) payment in food might be the only way to dispose of exotic surplus commodities which would find no market if sold in the normal way. The author concludes that somewhere between one-third and two-thirds of the cost of a public works programme could be met by the sale of food aid on the open market.

153.   MAXWELL, Simon. "Food Aid for Supplementary Feeding Programmes--An Analysis." *Food Policy* 3 (4): 289-298, November.

1978

An assessment of the nutritional impact of supplementary feeding programs and their costs and benefits. Suggests that the use of local foods to support supplementary feeding programs may be more beneficial than the use of food aid. Concludes that open market sales may be the best way to use food aid, "provided that local production is safeguarded by demand expansion and that complementary aid is available to prevent inflation in other sectors," and advises that "the use of food aid in supplementary feeding should be approached with caution."

154.   MAXWELL, Simon. "Tracing Feeding Programme Drop-outs." *Food Policy* 4 (1): 52-53, February.

1979

The importance of the drop-out rate of participants in supplemental food aid programs is related to the evaluation of the overall effectiveness of the food aid program in developing countries. Using data from a WFP project in Mexico, the author provides an exercise demonstrating the differences in results, depending on assumptions about drop-outs.

155. MAYER, Jean; and DWYER, Joanna. Food and Nutrition Policy in a Changing World. New York: Oxford University Press. 300 p.

1979

Emphasizing the need for close communication between nutritionists, economists and government planners, authors elucidate the need for comprehensive food and nutrition policy planning. Focus is on demand, supply and need considerations.

156. McHENRY, Dean E., Jr. Tanzania's Ujamaa Villages: The Implementation of a Rural Development Strategy. Berkeley, California: Institute of International Studies, University of California, Berkeley. 268 p.

1979

An assessment of the socialist Ujamaa village policy. Reports that within a decade of the policy's launching, 13,500,000 peasants (about 90% of the rural population) had moved into 7,300 villages. Describes the effects of this policy on agricultural development and production.

157. McNITT, Harold A. "French Farmers, Government Still Committed to EC's CAP." Foreign Agriculture 14 (9): 3-5, March 1.

1976

A discussion of France's agricultural policies and support of CAP. Concludes that the French farmer has a direct voice in French agricultural policy--and indirectly in the Common Market's policy--through an effective network of organizations.

158. MEAD, Arthur. "P. L. 480-Humanitarian Effort Helps Develop Markets." Foreign Agriculture 13 (32): 29, May 26.

1975

An explanation of how P. L. 480 contributes to the expansion of U. S. commercial agricultural sales. First, P. L. 480 agricultural products were introduced into foreign markets. Then new commercial relationships were established and promoted by U. S. trade through the cooperative foreign market development program partly funded with P.L. 480 revenues.

159. MELLOR, John W. "Food Price Policy and Income Distribution in Low-Income Countries." Economic Development and Cultural Change 27 (1): 1-26, October.

1978

Delineates the various effects of specific food price policies on income distribution on the basis of a general equilibrium analysis. Part I explores the effect of a change in relative food prices on the absolute and relative levels of income of various consumer classes. Part II shifts to the distributional effects of price changes on producers of different income classes. Part III examines the complex question of the effect of prices on agricultural production, first in the context of technological change. Part IV briefly presents a number of considerations relating food prices to employment in the agricultural and non-agricultural sectors. Part V summarizes major policy implications which may be drawn from the various partial analyses.

160. METTRICK, Hal. *Food Aid and Britain.* London: The Overseas Development Institute, Ltd. 124 p.

1969

Takes a brief look at the history of food aid and international agreements to provide food aid. Theoretically discusses the impact of food aid on domestic agricultural production in recipient countries and world trade based on the experience of three recipients: India, Pakistan and Israel. An additional section examines food aid policies and burden-sharing. "The principal conclusion is that for food aid to be an efficient way of transfering resources to developing countries there must be some mechanism for relating value of food aid to the recipient to its cost to the donor." Suggests that this can be best achieved by offering food aid as one of a number of interchangeable options within a complete aid package.

161. MIELKE, Myles. "New Argentine Policy Seen Basis of Gains in Farm Production." *Foreign Agriculture* 16 (1): 2-4, 12, January 2.

1978

Discusses Argentina's agricultural and food policies for the 1976/77 crop year. The country's strong agricultural economy is attributed to favorable government policies and good weather. Describes specific government projects.

162. MINEAR, Larry. "Development Aids for a Hungry World." *Christian Century.* 92 (28): 761-764, September.

1975

Describes the pros and cons of the International Development and Food Assistance Act of 1975 (H.R. 9005). Contends that this bill "more effectively integrated [food aid] into a unified program of international development and food assistance than it was in its political past."

163. MISSIAEN, Edmond. "Chile's New Agrarian Reform Policy May Help Boost Output." *Foreign Agriculture* 17 (39): 10-11, 16, September 30.

1974

Explains Chile's Agrarian reform law was one of many agricultural policies implemented in the early seventies to reverse the downward trend in farm production. Traces the evolution of Chilean agricultural reform policies and other policy goals such as encouragement of regional agricultural cooperatives and the promotion of rural-based industries which deal with the problem of inequity in the farm sector.

164. MITCHELL, Don. *The Politics of Food*. Toronto, Canada: James Lorrimer. 235 p.

1975

An analysis of the food industry and food price policy in Canada.

165. MORRIS, Roger, and SHEETS, Hal. *Disaster in the Desert: Failures of International Relief in the West African Drought*. Washington, D.C.: Carnegie Endowment for International Peace. 167 p.

1974

This study chronicles international food aid and emergency relief efforts taken during the Sahelian (West African region) drought crisis. It discusses a number of issues: the internal politics and bureaucratic rivalries within the international relief system; national and international food policies in an era when priorities between commercial purchases and humanitarian relief can be matters of life and death; and the responsibility of national legislatures for humane and responsive relief policies. The complete texts of various documents are included such as the Department of State Korry Report, the Center for Disease Control Nutritional Surveillance Reports and the 1973 Agency for International Development Report for the President on Emergency Disaster Relief and Sahel Africa.

166. MURRAY, Kenneth L. "Ivory Coast: Breakdown in Rice Program May Lead to Larger U.S. Sales." *Foreign Agriculture* 17 (21): 23-24, December.

1979

A description of the failure of the Ivory Coast's rice support policies, the stagnation of domestic production and the weak commercial collection system. The author predicts that the U.S. market share of Ivorian rice imports, already more than 50%, will rise significantly in the future.

167.   NATIONAL RESEARCH COUNCIL. <u>World Food and Nutrition Study:</u>
       <u>The Potential Contributions of Research</u>. Washington D.C.:
1977   National Academy of Sciences. 216 p.

   An examination of the dimensions of the world food and nutrition problem based on the work of over 200 international scientists, administrators and industrialists and five U.S. government agencies. Provides a useful compendium of facts on international agricultural trade, finance and food supply. For example, the report points out that: 1) in nine rapidly developing countries, imports of U.S. farm products increased 44 times between 1955 and 1973; and 2) a study of 66 countries showed that in 1957-64, as per capita income rose by 10%, agricultural imports rose by 25% in low-income countries and only 8% in high-income countries. High priority research areas are documented and a section on how to get the work done is included. The research is divided into four main areas: nutrition, food products, food marketing and policies and organizations.

168.   NAURIYA, A. K. "On the Agrarian Question in India."
       <u>Monthly Review</u> 30: 37-48, September.
1978

   Discusses food production and planning policies of India and calls for land reform to provide for better utilization of resources.

169.   NEUNTEUFEL, Marta. "Modelling Food and Agricultural Systems: A State-of-the-Art Study." <u>Food Policy</u> 4 (2):
1979   87-94, May.

   Based on a sample of about forty national and international models, the author provides a comprehensive survey of models which have been constructed to analyze factors in the field of food and agriculture. She briefly discusses grain reserve models and the third world Model of International Relations in Agriculture (MOIRA) which considers the balancing role of stockpiling activities and effects of food aid.

170.   NEVILLE-ROLFE, Edmund. <u>Economic Aspects of Agricultural</u>
       <u>Development in Africa: A Selective Annotated Reading List</u>
1969   <u>of Reports and Studies Concerning 40 African Countries During the Period 1960-1969</u>. Oxford: University of Oxford Agricultural Economics Research Institute. 264 p.

   Although the reference system of this bibliography is cumbersome, it contains valuable information on 1,394 studies examining the role of agriculture in economic development by country. Each country listing includes reference sources on: 1) National planning; 2) Regional studies; 3) Land tenure; 4) Co-operative forms of enterprise; 5) Capital and credit; 6) Livestock production; 7) Crop production; 8) Irrigation; 9) Marketing/consumption; 10) Processing industries; 11) Extension services and Community development; 12) Rural/urban relations; and 13) Statistical services. Emphasis is on thirty-seven African countries.

171.   NG, Gek-boo. "Incentive Policy in Chinese Collective Agriculture." Food Policy 4 (2): 75-86, May.

1979

Describes the provisions of China's agricultural incentive policy for rural collectives, and the impact of this policy on agricultural development. Details its mechanisms of taxes and fiscal incentives, price policies, subsidies, loans and technical assistance. Discusses the issues of food policy planning, agricultural growth, self-reliant development, and raising the marketed proportion of foodgrain output. Recommended food policy measures are: "1) to intensify foodgrain and agricultural production by allocating more manpower for rural infrastructure works and collective farming; 2) to increase state investment in agriculture to a 'very large extent'; 3) to extend research on agricultural technology and its diffusion; and 4) to accelerate the process of agricultural mechanization through the campaign of 'Learning from Tachai.'"

172.   NORTH AMERICAN CONGRESS ON LATIN AMERICA. "The Food for Peace Arsenal." NACLA Newsletter 5 (3): 1-7, May-June.

1971

Discusses the use of food aid for military purposes and U.S. use of counterpart funds generated from the sale of food aid in underdeveloped countries. Concludes that P. L. 480 works against local agrarian reform efforts and gives the U.S. increased capacity to manipulate and control under-developed economies.

173.   O'BRIEN, Andrew J.   "Does Food Aid Really Help?"   America 133 (11): 232-33, October 18.

1975

Describes how American food aid was used by Indian Villagers of Baliguma (near Tamshedpur, India) to grow enough food to feed themselves. The Food Marketing Center of Xavier School in Tamshedpur used food aid to teach villagers how to plan, build, maintain and share a common reservoir and flood-control facilities.

174.   OGURA, Takekazu. *Can Japanese Agriculture Survive?* Tokyo: Agricultural Policy Research Center. 850 p.
1979

An historical review of Japanese food and agricultural policy and analysis of its current condition.

175.   OECD. *Agricultural Policy in Australia.* Paris: OECD. 121 p.
1973

Description of Australia's agricultural policy as discussed and adopted by the OECD Working Party on Agricultural Policies, at a meeting on 29th January-2nd February, 1973.

176.   OECD. *Agricultural Policy in Austria.* Paris: OECD. 45 p.
1976   Contains a description of Austria's agricultural policies based on the OECD Working Party on Agricultural Policies meeting held 14th-18th October, 1974.

177.   OECD. *Agricultural Policy in Belgium.* Paris: OECD. 52 p.
1973   A description of Belgium's agricultural policies as adopted by the OECD Working Party on Agricultural Policies at a meeting on 25th-29th June, 1973.

178.   OECD. *Agricultural Policy in Canada.* Paris: OECD. 72 p.
1973   A discussion of Canada's agricultural policies as adopted by the OECD Working Party on Agricultural Policies at a meeting on 29th January-2nd February, 1973.

179.   OECD. *Agricultural Policy in Denmark.* Paris: OECD. 63 p.
1974   Synopsis of Denmark's agricultural policies as adopted by the OECD Working Party on Agricultural Policies, at a meeting on 18th-22nd February, 1974.

180.   OECD. *Agricultural Policy in Finland.* Paris: OECD. 51 p.
1975   Review of the state of agriculture in Finland and the agricultural policy objectives of the country. This is one of a series of agricultural policy reviews in 26 OECD member countries.

181.   OECD. <u>Agricultural Policy in France</u>. Paris: OECD. 87 p.

1974   Delineates the agricultural policies of France as adopted by the OECD Working Party on Agricultural Policies, at a meeting on 3rd-8th December 1973. Includes bibliographical references.

182.   OECD. <u>Agricultural Policy in Germany</u>. Paris: OECD. 59 p.

1974   Summary of Germany's agricultural policies as adopted by the OECD Working Party on Agricultural Policies, at a meeting on 3rd-8th December, 1973.

183.   OECD. <u>Agricultural Policy in Greece</u>. Paris: OECD. 53 p.

1973   Description of Greece's agricultural policies as adopted by the OECD Working Party on Agricultural Policies, at a meeting on 29th January-2nd February, 1973.

184.   OECD. <u>Agricultural Policy in Iceland</u>. Paris: OECD. 26 p.

1976   One of a series of reviews of agricultural policy in OECD member countries.

185.   OECD. <u>Agricultural Police in Ireland</u>. Paris: OECD. 62 p.

1974   Contains a description of Ireland's agricultural policies based on the OECD Working Party on Agricultural Policies meeting held 18th-22nd February, 1974.

186.   OECD. <u>Agricultural Policy in Italy</u>. Paris: OECD. 53 p.

1973   A review of Italy's agricultural policies as adopted by the OECD Working Party on Agricultural Policies, at a meeting on 25th-29th June, 1973.

187.   OECD. <u>Agricultural Policy in Japan</u>. Paris: OECD. 80 p.

1974   Report adopted by the OECD Working Party on Agricultural Policies, at a meeting on 3rd-8th December, 1973.

188.   OECD. <u>Agricultural Policy in Luxemburg</u>. Paris: OECD. 33 p.

1974   A discussion of agricultural policies in Luxemburg presented by the OECD Working Party on Agricultural Policy.

189. OECD. <u>Agricultural Policy in the Netherlands.</u> Paris: OECD. 60 p.

1973

One of a series of reports of OECD member country's agricultural policies. Adopted by the OECD Working Party on Agricultural Policies on 25th-29th June, 1973.

190. OECD. <u>Agricultural Policy in New Zealand.</u> Paris: OECD. 93 p.

1974

One of a series of reveiws of agricultural policy in member countries.

191. OECD. <u>Agricultural Policy in Norway.</u> Paris: OECD. 46 p.

1975 The agricultural policy objectives and specific programs of Norway are reviewed. This is one of a series of agricultural policy reviews in 26 OECD member countries.

192. OECD. <u>Agricultural Policy in Portugal.</u> Paris: OECD. 44 p.

1975 One of a series of 26, this volume examines the state of agriculture and agricultural policy aims and measures in Portugal.

193. OECD. <u>Agricultural Policy in Spain.</u> Paris: OECD. 49 p.

1974 One of a series of reviews of agricultural policy in OECD member countries.

194. OECD. <u>Agricultural Policy in Sweden.</u> Paris: OECD. 58 p.

1974 Description of Sweden's agricultural policies as adopted by the OECD Working Party on Agricultural Policies, at a meeting on 10th-13th June, 1974.

195. OECD. <u>Agricultural Policy in Switzerland.</u> Paris: OECD. 79 p.

1973

Report of the OECD Working Party on Agricultural Policies on Switzerland's agricultural policies.

196. OECD. <u>Agricultural Policy in Turkey.</u> Paris: OECD. 60 p.

1974 Summary of Turkey's agricultural policies as adopted by the

OECD Working Party on Agricultural Policies, on 18th-22nd February, 1974.

197. OECD. <u>Agricultural Policy in the United Kingdom</u>. Paris: OECD. 66 p.

1974

Agricultural policies in the United Kingdom are described.

198. OECD. <u>Agricultural Policy in the United States</u>. Paris: OECD. 106 p.

1974

One of a series of reviews of agricultural policy in OECD member countries.

199. OECD. <u>Agricultural Policy in Yugoslavia</u>. Paris: OECD. 47 p.

1973

Description of Yugoslavia's agricultural policies as adopted by the OECD Working Party on Agricultural Policies on 29th January-2nd February, 1973.

200. OECD. <u>Agricultural Policy of the European Economic Community</u>. Paris: OECD. 118 p.

1974

Agricultural policies of the EEC are outlined by the OECD Working Party on Agricultural Policies.

201. OECD. <u>Development Assistance: Efforts and Policies of the Members of the Development Assistance Committee, 1968 Review</u>, by Edwin M. Martin. Paris: OECD. 278 p.

1968

Chapter VIII, "Aid, Agricultural Development and Population Policy," explains the relationship between agricultural development and food assistance.

202. OECD. <u>Development Assistance: Efforts and Policies of the Members of the Development Assistance Committee, 1971 Review</u>, by Edwin M. Martin. Paris: OECD. 203 p.

1971

Chapter V examines some of the problems of food aid and their implications for future aid policies. Topics discussed include the types of food aid, the terms of food aid and the current volume of food aid programs.

203.   OECD. *Development Co-operation: Efforts and Policies of the Members of the Development Assistance Committee, 1974 Review*, by Maurice Williams. Paris: OECD. 325 p.

1974

Focuses on the effects of oil price changes and food shortages on development. Chapter V provides an assessment of the role of food aid in development including a review of the principal characteristics of food aid; the principal problems raised by food aid; the case for food aid; and possible improvements in food aid policies and programs. Provides a brief description of the food situation, emergency food aid in the Sahel, world food security, national storage policies in developing countries, international agricultural adjustment policy and development assistance for food production in the developing countries.

204.   OECD. *Development Co-operation: Efforts and Policies of the Members of the Development Assistance Committee, 1975 Review*, by Maurice Williams. Paris: OECD. 261 p.

1975

Focusing on the importance of the rural sector and the needs of non-oil developing countries, this report reviews the impact of OECD member country development aid. Chapter IV contains a synopsis of agricultural development plans and policies in the following countries: Peru, Mexico, Argentina, India, Philippines, Malaysia, Algeria, Morocco, Tunisia and Kenya.

205.   OECD. *Development Co-operation: Efforts and Policies of the Members of the Development Assistance Committee, 1976 Review*, by Maurice Williams. Paris: OECD. 273 p.

1976

Appraisal of the development assistance policies and programs of OECD member nations. Chapter VI discusses the volume and terms of aid, the sectoral distribution of agricultural assistance, the geographic distribution of food aid and the need for better food aid programming. The report concludes that: 1) food aid policy must insure that funded projects are capable of responding more directly to the needs of poorer groups; 2) food aid should be provided over several years; and 3) food aid should be more closely linked to agricultural development projects. Provides a lengthy review of agricultural development stratagies for the Sahel.

206.   OECD. *Food Aid*. Paris: OECD. 134 p.

1974

An important contribution of the OECD Secretariat to the international discusson on food aid to developing countries. Study consists of: 1) a general note on the features and the problems of food aid, as well as the case for it; 2) an annex containing individual notes on the food aid programs of OECD Development Assistance Committee Members; and 3) a statistical annex. Topics discussed include: geographic distribution of food aid, repercussions of food aid on international trade, management problems of food aid and food aid versus financial assistance.

207. OECD. <u>Food Aid: Its Role in Economic Development</u>. Paris: OECD. 85 p.

1964

Considers the long-term economic implications of food aid, describes basic food aid principles and delineates ways in which food aid can be used to promote economic development. Examines the experience gained under food aid programs including P. L. 480, the Mutual Security Program, the Colombo Plan and Canadian and French programs. Discusses the problems which may arise for the agricultural economy of the receiving country, for world trade and for the donor country. This leads to a discussion of the future of food aid emphasizing relationships between food aid and other forms of aid.

208. OECD. <u>Food Aid for Development</u>, by Hartmut Schneider. Rome: OECD. 130 p.

1979

Report on the food aid findings of the OECD Development Centre Expert Meeting, Paris, March 30-31, 1978.

209. OECD. <u>Review of Agricultural Policies 1977</u>. Paris: OECD. 126 p.

1978

Report on OECD Member Countries' agricultural policy developments and responses during 1976-77. Describes food aid policies and the agricultural policies of the developing nations in relation to their impact on OECD countries.

210. OECD. <u>Review of Agricultural Policies in OECD Member Countries 1974-76</u>. Paris: OECD. 115 p.

1977

Interprets OECD Member Countries' agricultural policy responses from the beginning of 1974 to the end of 1976. Contains an analysis and assessment of agricultural policy measures on agricultural incomes, supply management, structural developments and agricultural trade. Provides country notes on specific policy developments and measures in Canada, New Zealand, Japan, France, Germany, Norway, Sweden and the United States.

211. OECD. Review of Agricultural Policies in OECD Member Countries, 1978. Rome: OECD. 141 p.

1979

OECD's Agricultural Policy Reports Series. Provides an analysis of agricultural policy measures taken in OECD member countries and information on the 1977 International Sugar Agreement.

212. OECD. Review of Agricultural Policies in OECD Member Countries, 1979. Rome: OECD. 116 p.

1980

Reviews trends and new developments in agricultural policies during 1979 and the performance of the agricultural sector within the general economy. Analyzes problem areas and provides country examples of most relevant measures.

213. OECD. Review of Agricultural Policies: General Survey. Paris: OECD. 103 p.

1975

Summary of the main policy issues confronting OECD Member Countries. Provides a comprehensive description of agricultural policy within the OECD orbit and describes the background against which policies are set and have to operate. Discusses major policy objectives and fields of policy actions focusing on price policy and the effect of world markets and trade policies on agricultural policy.

214. OECD. Special Annotated Bibliography: Agricultural Policy, Vols. 27 and 28. Paris: OECD. 162 p. and 238 p. respec-
1970   tively.

Listings of studies on agricultural policy problems of OECD member countries. Emphasizes the theory of agricultural policy and the Common Agricultural Policy of the EEC.

215. OECD. The Food Problem of Developing Countries. Paris, OECD. 114 p.

1968

A study of how member countries of the OECD can contribute to the "co-ordination of bilateral and of international programmes aimed at increasing food production and improving nutritional levels in the developing countries . . . " Analyzes demand and supply factors for food and production in developing countries from 1965-80. Discusses the relationship between mounting imports, debt servicing problems and agricultural development based on food aid and trade policies. Recommends the increase of food and development aid "under conditions which will encourage governments of and farmers in the developing countries to take measures to increase their own agricultural activity."

216.   OECD/FAO. Critical Issues on Food Marketing Systems in Developing Countries: Report of the OECD/FAO Joint Seminar,
1977   Paris, 18-22, October, 1976. Paris: OECD. 97 p.

Discusses the nature and degree of government food marketing policies and services, government grain price policies and small farmer orientation to government policies. Reviews options for international food assistance.

217.   PAYNE, P. R. "Nutrition Planning and Food Policy." Food Policy 1 (2): 107-115, February.
1976

Describes the relationships between nutrition and development planning. Contends that recent development priorities may be a cause of malnutrition in poor countries. Examines factors affecting food policy in developing countries and calls for an interdisciplinary approach to planning.

218.   PECK, Anne E., and GRAY, Roger W. "Grain Reserves—Unresolved Issues." Food Policy 5 (1): 26-37, February.
1980

Points to three important issues relative to optimal grain stockpiling policies: 1) the role of private stockholding and its relationship to publicly held (or subsidized) reserves; 2) the nature and export demand for U.S. wheat and its relationship to reserves proposals; and 3) the distribution of (wheat) crop yields as it may bear upon the functioning of a reserves plan. Argues that the success of any proposed scheme and the formulation of appropriate policy depends significantly on the resolution of these issues.

219.   PENN, J.B., and BOEHM, W.T. "Research Issues Re-emphasized by 1977 Food Policy Legislation." Agricultural Economics
1978   Research 30 (1): 1-14. January.

Summarizes food policy research issues and their relation to the formulation of US food policy.

220.   PHILLIPS, Don, and COOLIDGE, Frank A.   "New Food Aid Convention Negotiated."   *Foreign Agriculture*   17 (5): 36, May.

1980

Under the 1980 Food Aid Convention developing countries will receive increased food aid and additional benefits. Gains includes: 1) rice is now formally allowed to fulfill obligations; 2) members will make their contributions ($7.6 million pledged), as far as possible on a forward planning basis; and 3) if low-income developing countries as a whole suffer a substantial shortfall in food grains, the Food Aid Committee (the United States, Canada, Australia, Argentina, Japan, the European Community and five other West European Countries) may recommend that members should increase the amount of aid available to cover emergency needs. This agreement replaces the Food Aid Convention of 1971 and falls considerably short of the World Food Conference target of at least 10 million tons of food aid annually to developing countries in the form of wheat and other grains.

221.   PINSTRUP-ANDERSEN, Per, and TWEETEN, Luther G.   "The Value, Cost, and Efficiency of American Food Aid."   *American Journal of Agricultural Economics*,   53 (3): 431-440, August.

1971

Develops a conceptual framework to estimate: 1) the value to recipient countries of food aid relative to untied cash aid and the value of U.S. food aid; 2) the cost to the donor countries of food aid relative to the best alternative outlet for surplus commodities and to estimate the cost of U.S. food aid; and 3) the social gain associated with food aid programs and food aid distribution between donor and recipient countries for 1964-66. Provides empirical estimates of the real costs and benefits for the three major types of U.S. food aid (grants, credit sales, and non-convertible curency sales) and for the total actual 1964-1966 aid.

222.   "The Politics of Food."   *Time Magazine*, March 17, p. 6.

1975   Short summary of the political maneuvering behind the delay in the 1975 fiscal year food aid program. The report states that "Congress wanted the supplies to go primarily to the 32 countries designated by the United Nations as those 'most severely affected' by famine, while the White House wanted to give special attention to the needs of Cambodia and South Viet Nam, although they were not on the U.N. list." The summary explains that even though Congress won the battle, the Administration added one million dollars to the food aid program to cover its commitments to Cambodia and South Viet Nam.

223. POLOPOLUS, L. "Food Prices and Policies: Some Domestic and International Aspects." Staff Paper Series, No. 33.
1976   Florida: University of Florida, Food and Resource Economics Department. 17 p.

Discusses the impact of U.S. domestic and international food policy on food price formation and the agro-industrial sector of the U.S.

224. POSPELOVA, E. "Reserves for Increasing Food Resources." Soviet Review. 17: 70-87, Winter.
1976-77

Discusses policy objectives affecting the utilization of agricultural reserves in the Soviet Union. Integrated agricultural and food policies discussed from a socialist perspective.

225. PRESIDENTIAL COMMISSION ON WORLD HUNGER. Preliminary Report of the Presidential Commission on World Hunger. Washington, D.C.: Presidential Commission on World Hunger.
1979   74 p.

Provides recommendations on broad actions and policies pertaining to U.S. relationships with developing countries, U.S. development assistance, famine relief and U.S. domestic hunger programs. Concludes that "if decisions and actions well within the capability of nations and people working together were implemented, it would be possible to eliminate the worst aspects of hunger and malnutrition by the year 2000."

226. RAO, V.K.R.V. Growth with Justice in Asian Agriculture: An Exercise in Policy Formulation. Geneva: United Nations
1974   Reserach Institute. 96 p.

Combines agricultural development with social justice on the basis of new technology and appropriate social, economic and organizational measures. Describes agricultural price policies and the trade-offs between rural and agricultural development in the Asian context.

227. RASTYANNIKOV, V. G. Food for Developing Countries in Asia and North Africa: A Socio-Economic Approach. New York:
1976   Arno Press. 104 p.

Discusses the main disproportion in the food balance of the developing nations particularly those factors affecting economic growth associated with the "critical state of the productive forces of agriculture." Proposes: 1) "possible ways of overcoming the dependence of the developing nations on the food supplies from the highly developed capitalist countries"; and 2) a strategic approach to reorganizing agriculture and peasant farming.

228. RATH, Nilakanth, and PATVERDHAN, V. S. Impact of Assistance and PL 480 on Indian Economy. Poona, Bombay: Gokhale In-
1967 stitute of Politics and Economics. 204 p.

USDA study analyzing the short- and long-term effects of P. L. 480 on Indian economic development from 1956-1962. Concludes that the program: 1) has helped the government hold the price of wheat at an artificially low, unchanging level; 2) did not adversely impact the area under cultivation and quantities produced; and 3) affected government policy by creating "a psychology of abundance" leading to unwillingness to promote adequate measures to substitute longer-run domestic production for food imports. P.L. 480 can only be a significant contributor to development if: 1) realistic price policies are established; and 2) government policies emphasize increased domestic food production.

229. RINGEN, K. "Norwegian Food and Nutrition Policy." American Journal of Public Health 67: 550-1, June.
1977

Short summary of the history of national and international food policy movements and the nutritional needs of its population.

230. ROGERS, Keith D.; SRIVASTAVA, Uma K; and HEADY, Earl O. "Modified Price, Production, and Income Impacts of Food Aid
1972 Under Market Differentiated Distribution." American Journal of Agricultural Economics 54 (2): 201-208, May.

"Estimation of negative production impacts of food aid rests heavily on measurement of resulting price changes. Previous studies have assumed exogenous shift in supply resulting from distribution of the imported commodities but have ignored the income effect on demand. Distribution of food aid commodities to consumers at concessional prices provides an increase in real income and corresponding shift in the demand for food." The authors show that: 1) a shift in demand compensates for part of the exogenous shift in supply, reducing the potential impact on domestic prices; and 2) based on market differentiation, the production impact in India was most likely one-tenth of previous estimates.

231. RUNGE, Carlisle Ford. "American Agricultural Assistance and the New International Economic Order." World Development 5 (8):. 725-746, August.

1977

Uses ethical political and economic arguments, and John Rawl's theory of distributive justice to describe the relationship between United States food aid and the Third World's call for a new international economic order. The United States slow development of a coherent policy relationship between agriculture, food aid, foreign affairs and the demands for a new international order has left developing countries with the sense that America's commitment to redistribution and economic equality is hypocritical. Suggests that "the best way to help the developing countries is to cut back on [American] food aid and agricultural assistance, and introduce policies designated to effect a more equitable world distribution of income. . . . This will require the acceptance of a distributive global contract, in which the self-interest of the United States is redefined in the context of longer-term interests and perspectives than may seem politically feasible even to the most far-sighted and moral of statesmen."

232. RUSSELL, Paul H. Food for Development in Sub-Sahara Africa. (Typewritten, unpublished Report) Washington, D.C.: Africa Bureau, Agency for International Development, AFR/DR/ARD 68 p.

1979

Draft report of the AID. Discusses food availability and P. L. 480 in Sub-Sahara Africa. Outlines a new food aid priority ranking procedure for consideration and possible use by the Africa Bureau of AID. Prioritizes Sub-Saharan food aid recipients according to their food needs and ability to utilize food aid for development.

233. SABATINI, Omero. "EC Reviews Its Farm Policy, Some Changes Expected." Foreign Agriculture 14 (9): 2-3, 6, March 1.

1976

Review of a report released by the EC Ministers of Agriculture in 1975. Highlights assessments made about EC agricultural policies, specifically CAP. Discusses EC price proposals, support policies, consumer and export policies and actions to improve productivity.

234. SABLE, Martin H. *Latin American Agriculture.* Milwaukee, Wisconsin: The University of Wisconsin. 74 p.

1970

Includes monographs and reference books, government publications, mainly in Spanish and Portuguese, but also in English, French, German and Italian. Emphasizes agricultural history and development policies from Discovery until 1969.

235. SAHEL DOCUMENTATION CENTER. *Sahel Bibliographic Bulletin/ Bulletin Bibliographique*, Vols 1-2. East Lansing, Michigan: Michigan State University.

1977-1978

Summarizes books, articles, papers and documents dealing with various aspects of agricultural and economic development in the Sahel. Provides notes on research projects and profiles of information centers.

236. SANDERSON, Fred H. "The Great Food Fumble." *Science* 188 (4188): 503-509, 9 May.

1975

The author contends that food aid should complement longer-term agricultural development. He suggests: "Properly administered food aid programmes can make an important contribution to economic development. There is ample evidence that undernourishment is a major factor in the low level of human productivity in many developing countries. And there are several ways in which food aid can be linked directly with rural community projects and other agricultural development activities."

237. SANDERSON, Fred H. *Japan's Food Prospects and Policies.* Washington, D.C.: The Brookings Institution. 99 p.

1978

Despite high rates of agricultural growth, Japan's dependence on foreign wheat imports increased rising to twenty million metric tons of wheat in 1972. The world grain crisis of 1972-73 led to the establishment of food policies emphasizing self-sufficiency. Discusses the pros and cons of these policies. Concludes that the new policies are neither wise nor feasible because: 1) there are likely to be considerable problems in obtaining target levels of roughage and cereal production in spite of generous support prices; and 2) Japanese estimates of the income elasticity of demand for meat are probably low and may lead to low demand estimates for feed grains.

238. SANDERSON, Fred H. "Next Steps on Grain Reserves." *Food Policy* 2 (4): 267-276, November.

1977

Examines American views on grain reserves and the policies of the Carter and Ford Administrations with respect to international wheat agreements and responsibilities. Discusses major issues to be resolved such as the scope of the reserve, farmer-held reserves, price incentives and the role of food aid in helping poor countries to carry their share of the reserve.

239. SANDERSON, Fred H. "The World Food Problem: Possibilities of International Action," Current History, 68 (406):
1975   265-270 and 276-8, June.

"For the first time in the history of mankind, the eradication of hunger and malnutrition has become a practical possibility." Consequently, ". . . the governments of the developing countries [must] redirect their domestic priorities toward the rural sector, whose backwardness, in many cases, has become the major constraint on their general economic development." Concludes that food aid should supplement agricultural development assistance to achieve maximum agricultural production in developing countries and provides examples for maximum effectiveness of food aid programs.

240. SCHERTZ, Lyle P. "World Food: Prices and the Poor." Foreign Affairs, 52 (3): 511-537, April.
1974

Compiles background data on international food production and consumption trends in developed and developing countries. Raises questions about international food policy, the role of the United States and the U.S.S.R. in alleviating the food deficits of the poor nations, and the need for food stockpiling and price stabilization. Concludes that "neither we (United States) nor other rich countries are willing to forgo substantial foreign exchange earnings in the interest of feeding the poor, even though the developing countries have only limited resources to do it themselves." Thus, P. L. 480 food aid to poor countries will most likely decrease in accordance with commercial self-interests of the United States. Encourages the world and the United States to evaluate trade-offs between food aid and other economic assistance."

241. SCHMITT, Bernard A. Protein, Calories, and Development: Nutritional Variables in the Economics of Developing Countries.
1979   Boulder, Colorado: Westview Press, Inc. 224 p.

Integrates economic analyses with concepts of nutritional science to provide an effective means for analyzing complex problems of agricultural production in nutritionally deficient nations. Traces circular relationship between nutrition, human capital, labor productivity, food production, and per capita consumption of calories and protein. Defines the basic nutritional terms that are most useful to economists and stresses the importance of nutritional quality and gross quantity. Uses a flexible methodology for forecasting commodity production to make projections for major commodity groups of developing nations and to test various policy alternatives such as extensive trade, expanded food assistance programs, substantial resource or input expansion, further expansion of Green Revolution technology, and development of alternatives to agriculture. Concludes that conditions in nutritionally deficient countries are unlikely to improve, on average, through the mid-1980's.

242. SCHNEIDER, Hartmut. *The Effects of Food Aid on Agricultural Production in Recipient Countries: An Annotated Selective Bibliography.* Paris: OECD. 41 p.

1975

Focuses only on reports or articles written between 1964 and 1975 dealing with the impact of food aid on the agricultural production of recipient countries. Contains 63 entries of books, articles and reports written in English, French or German. Includes a summary review of the major arguments and underlying assumptions of the direct and indirect effects of food aid.

243. SCHNEIDER, Hartmut. *Food Aid for Development.* Paris: Development Centre of the OECD 130 p.

1978

Highlights the 1978 OECD Development Centre Expert Meeting on "Scope and Conditions for Improved Use of Food Aid for Development." Two basic hypotheses underly the findings: 1) food aid has a development potential beyond what has conventionally been made use of; and 2) past experience shows the scope and conditions under which improvements in food aid planning and operations could possibly be achieved. Issues addressed include the trade-offs between food aid and other types of aid, the impact of food aid on production, the controversy on counterpart funds, food aid coordination and donor constraints. Suggests that: 1) what can be achieved with food aid supplies depends largely on the development strategies pursued by the recipient countries; 2) conflicts between output and distribution objectives of food aid can be resolved; and 3) complementary assistance provides for a fuller use of food aid for development.

244. SCHNEIDER, Hartmut. "Review and Prospects of German Food Aid for Selected Asian Countries." In Food Aid for Development, pp. 60-68. Edited by Hartmut-Schneider. Paris: Development Centre of the OECD.

1978

A general discussion of the food aid program of Germany in Bangladesh, Indonesia, Pakistan and Sri Lanka from 1971-1974. Provides country-specific data, but for reasons of confidentiality, the countries concerned are not always identified in the text. Examines the effects of food aid on local production, the availability of bulk food aid, cooperation between donor and recipient countries, projected food aid supplies and food for work projects. Enumerates specific food aid recommendations for Sri Lanka and Bangladesh.

245. SCHNEIDER, William Jr. "Agricultural Exports as an Instrument of Diplomacy." Food Policy 1 (1): 23-31, November.

1975

Assesses the role that agricultural exports could play in US foreign policy and concludes that "it could have significant short-term impacts and would counter-balance attempts by other producers to interrupt exports of their indigenous raw materials."

246. SCHNEIDER, William. Food, Foreign Policy, and Raw Materials Cartels. New York: Crane, Russak & Co. 122 p.

1976

Analyzes the potential of agricultural commodities as an instrument of United States foreign policy with particular emphasis on its "economic warfare" potential.

247. SCHUH, Dr. G. Edward. "The Effects of Food Aid." Foreign Agriculture 17 (13): 5-8, April.

1979

Contains the highlights of a speech by the author. Discusses American food aid programs, their direction, implementation, problems and impact. Addresses fundamental questions about the relationship of food aid to: 1) the creation of dependency on the part of the recipient; 2) the improvement of the nutritional status of the very poor; 3) the maintenance of U.S. trade and policy aims; and 4) the formation of human capital and improvement in incomes.

248. SCHULTZ, Theodore W. "Value of U. S. Farm Surpluses to Underdeveloped Countries." Journal of Farm Economics 42 (5): 1019-1030, December.

1960

An analysis of the effect of American food aid on underdeveloped countries. A pioneering effort in testing the effectiveness of P.L. 480 with theoretical economic tools. Predicted long-run adverse effects of P.L. 480 on underdeveloped countries.

249.   SCHWARZ, Reinhold. "Swiss Goal: Increased Food Self-Sufficiency." *Foreign Agriculture* 16 (41): 8-10, October 9.
1978

Discusses Switzerland's national policies and commitment to a high level of food self-sufficiency. Suggests that these policies "could result in declining markets for U.S. grain."

250.   SEEVERS, Gary L. "An Evaluation of the Disincentive Effect Caused by P.L. 480 Shipments." *American Journal of Agri-*
1968   *cultural Economics*, 50 (3): 630-642, August.

Evaluates the likely magnitudes of the disincentive effect of P.L. 480 based on an analysis of price-output relationships. Suggests: "Changes in foodgrain prices and domestic output caused by changing the quality of U.S. Public Law 480 shipments to a hypothetical country show that both prices and output are highly sensitive to elasticities of supply and demand." But for many cases examined, changes in these shipments had relatively insignificant price output effects and these could have been offset by a modest growth in population. Estimates of parameters for India indicate "that a 20 percent increase in the quantity of foodgrain shipments between 1956-57 and 1961-62, other things being equal, would have decreased foodgrain prices 1.6 percent and domestic foodgrain output 0.4 percent. These disincentives may be outweighed by the effects on consumption, income distribution, and resource allocation, suggesting that, overall, the effects of P.L. 480 shipments are beneficial."

251.   SELECT COMMITTEE ON OVERSEAS DEVELOPMENT. *The World Food Crisis and Third World Development: Implications for U. K.*
1976   *Policy.* HMSO, London, UK: Select Committee on Overseas Development: 370 p.

Includes the proceedings of the committee. Suggests major structural changes in England's pattern of food aid giving to ensure successful rural development.

252.   SEN, S. R. "Impact and Implications of Foreign Surplus Disposal on Underdeveloped Economies." *Journal of Farm*
1960   *Economics* 42 (5): 1031-1042, December.

Discusses the impact of P.L. 480 on the Indian economy from 1955-59 from the vantage point of the recipient.

253. SEN, S. R. "Whither Aid?" American Journal of Agricultural Economics 53 (5): 768-776, December.

1971

Analyzes the impact of P.L. 480 food aid on India and argues that US P.L. 480 wheat sales "have not adversely affected wheat production in India." Contends that governmental policies prevented disincentive effects because it took measures to insure food aid did not discourage domestic food production from the onset of P.L. 480 deliveries.

254. SHAW, D. J. Agricultural Develompment in the Sudan, Vol. 1 & 2. Khartoum, Sudan: Philosophical Society of the Sudan. 171 p. and 494 p. respectively.

1965

Discusses the role of agriculture in Sudan's economic development based on the proceedings of the thirteenth annual conference of the Philosophical Society of the Sudan in conjunction with the Sudan Agricultural Society. Contains policy statements and reports of various government agencies, officials and international experts on the problems of Sudanese agricultural development.

255. SHEFRIN, Frank. "Multilateral Food Aid and Development, A Decade of WFP Operations." Agriculture Abroad 27 (2): 37-57, April.

1973

A review of WFP activities. Discusses the disincentive impacts of food aid on production. Concludes that this effect "is possible where food aid is very large in terms of a country's requirements, but the WFP resources are not sufficient for this to occur."

256. SHEFRIN, Frank. "The World Food Programme, Aid for Development." Canadian Farm Economics 6 (5): 8-21, December.

1971

A general survey article on WFP development aid. Concludes that WFP food aid promotes agricultural development "by supporting projects for improvement and investment in agriculture."

257. SHENOY, B. R. "Aid to India Under the United States Public Law 480." Indian Journal of Economics (Allahabad, India) 52 (206): 211-241, January.

1972

Contends that industrialized nations will continue to dump surpluses in the form of food aid on developing nations as long as the recipient country's price support policies favor it. Examines the impact of food aid on domestic food production and on governmental policies.

258. SHENOY, Bellikoth Raghunath. *P. L. 480 Aid and India's Food Problem*. New Delhi: Affiliated East-West Press, PVT. LTD.
1974 342 p.

Delineates the impact of P.L. 480 food aid in India. Examines the economic effects of P.L. 480 imports, the monetary consequences of P.L. 480 finance and provides an analysis of the impact of the P.L. 480 policy objective of self-help in relation to effective demand. A critical review of the inflationary effects of P.L. 480 is followed by a discussion of the 1974 Rupee Settlement Agreement. Points out the relationships between P. L. 480 aid and: 1) nutrition deficits; 2) capital starvation of agriculture; and 3) economic development. Describes food policy measures of the Indian government. Concludes that P.L. 480 food imports and other concessional imports will continue unless there is a restructuring of overall economic policies.

259. SHUMAN, Charles B. "Food Aid and the Free Market." In *Food Policy: The Responsibility of the United States in
1977 the Life and Death Choices*, pp. 145-163. Edited by Peter G. Brown and Henry Shue. New York: The Free Press.

Examines some of the causes of hunger and the possibility of using the free market approach toward correcting food imbalances. Evaluates present food aid programs and suggests modifications which encourage greater free market action. Concludes that "[t]he free competitive market is the only device that will provide the discipline and the incentives necessary to cause undernourished people to solve their own problems."

260. SINGER, H. W. "A Summary Survey of Studies of Food Aid;" In *Food Aid for Development*, pp. 43-49. Edited by H.
1978 Schneider. Paris: Development Centre of the OECD.

A review of the food aid literature "dealing with the impact of food aid on local food production and on government policies and its role in support of labour-intensive works and nutritional improvement." Emphasizes qualifiable economic studies. Draws general food policy conclusions based on the review which should help governments to establish "policy guidelines that will gear food aid more closely to nutrition, production, employment and other development objectives, in line with the recommendation of the World Food Council at its Third Session in June 1977." Challenges critics of food aid programs and advocates distribution of food aid through differentiated channels "because of its effectiveness in reducing downward pressures on food prices and because it can be used to reach specific target groups: the poor, the unemployed, the undernourished."

261. SINHA, Radha. *Food and Poverty: The Political Economy of Confrontation.* New York: Holmes & Meier Publishers. 196 p.

1976

Argues that the problem of world hunger and poverty is leading to a crisis between rich and poorer countries because at both the national and international level there is a "reluctance to take a realistic view of the alternatives available in the fight against poverty, unemployment and malnutrition." Advocates a more equitable, international income distribution and the formulation of non-palliative food and agricultural policies as a pre-requisite for meaningful development. Discusses alternative means of increasing food production. The multilateralisation of food aid may provide greater food security for developing nations, but, it "does not provide a watertight guarantee that food aid will not be used as a political weapon." Discusses relevant findings of the 1974 World Food Conference in Rome pursuant to the future of food aid.

262. SISAYE, Seleshi; and STOMMES, Eileen. "Agricultural Development in Ethiopia: Government Budgeting and Development Assistance in the Pre and Post 1975 Periods." *The Journal of Development Studies* 16 (2): 156-185, January.

1980

An comprehensive analysis of Ethiopian agricultural development policies from the First Five Year Plan (1957-61) to the present. Describes the role of foreign assistance and the effectiveness of agricultural development projects sponsored by various countries and agencies such as the World Bank and USAID. Concludes that foreign aid has played a significant role in agricultural development programs since 1967 and has indirectly contributed to Ethiopian rural development "by providing a trial-and-error basis of agricultural development experience, and initiating the necessary rural development infrastructure."

263. SOBEL, Lester A., editor. *World Food Crisis.* New York: Facts on File. 172 p.

1975

Chronicles information about a wide variety of issues related to the international food problem. Summarizes specific food aid and relief efforts in countries such as Bangladesh, India, Pakistan, Biafra, Ethiopia and the Sahel. Includes texts of the Declaration and of the 22 resolutions adopted by the 1974 World Food Conference.

264. SORENSON, Vernon L. <u>International Trade Policy: Agriculture and Development</u>. East Lansing, Michigan: Michigan
1975 State University. 290 p.

Intended for classroom use. Provides an analysis of international agricultural market conditions and the formulation of trade policy. Explains how "the domestic agricultural policies of the advanced nations are aimed at protection, while those of the less advanced are directed toward exploitation of agriculture in the interest of foreign exchange savings and economic development." Includes a brief discussion of the United States P.L. 480 program. Contends that it: 1) "reduced the need for supply control programs and changed the emphasis between demand expansion and supply control as vehicles for overcoming the imbalance created by agricultural protection . . ."; and 2) enhanced U.S. political interest by representing "an initial interaction with some socialist countries, which, over time, have become more closely oriented toward Western commercial interests."

265. SORENSON, Vernon L.; and HAMM, Larry G. "Food and Food Policy in the Industrial Nations." <u>Current History</u>, 68
1975 (406): 241-244, 273-4, June.

Contends that since developed countries "dominate the production of food, their policy choices directly affect the less advantaged people of the world. . . . Western food-sufficient nations must examine and direct their food policies towards programs that will stabilize world markets, promote efficiency in the use of agricultural resources, and benefit less developed countries." Enumerates three major policy issues: 1) international agricultural adjustment and improvement of the effectiveness of world agricultural resource use; 2) structural imbalances in the international food situation (e.g. availability of foreign exchange reserves); and 3) food security and stabilization to deal with unforseen shortages.

266. SRIVASTAVA, Uma Kant. "The Impact of Public Law 480 Imports on Prices and Domestic Supply of Cereals in India: Comment." *American Journal of Agricultural Economics* 50 (1): 143-145, February.

1968

A critique of Jitendar S. Mann's article, "The Impact of Public Law 480 Imports on Prices and Domestic Supply of Cereals in India." Contrary to the conclusions of Mann, Srivastava contends that "the food problem will grow more acute if P.L. 480 supplies cause a decline in domestic production, no matter whether it is more or less than proportionate to imports, for it will increasingly widen the gap between the demand and domestic supply, defeating the very purpose of food aid." Discusses the difference between prices at fair price shops and prices in the open market. Concludes that food "prices not only be prevented from falling but actually can be kept at a higher level despite P.L. 480 imports through the working of the fair price shops."

267. SRIVASTAVA, Uma K., in collaboration with HEADY, Earl O.; ROGERS, Keith D.; and MAYER, Leo V. *Food Aid and International Economic Growth*. Ames, Iowa: The Iowa State University Press. 160 p.

1975

The implications of this valuable study far exceed the case of its reference country, India. The empirical analysis highlights "the relevance of the food constraint in the context of the growth process." Examines critical issues regarding the efficiency of food aid as a tool for economic development such as: 1) "negative price and production impact on domestic producers in recipient countries; 2) hardening of the terms of food aid and lowering of aid component in the shipments; and 3) solution of problems associated with the excess accumulation and utilization of counterpart funds out of past aid agreements." Contains an authoritative treatment of the "Price Disincentive Effect in Recipient Countries." Makes an assessment of "potentials and prospects of using food aid for additional economic development." Concludes that the future development use of food aid is limited unless the policies of both the United States and recipients change. Includes a very useful Appendix A, "Review of Related Studies" including: 1) the Food and Agriculture Organization Pilot Study of India; 2) Michigan State Study of Colombia; 3) USDA Study of United Arab Republic; 4) USDA Study of Turkey; and 5) Arizona Study of Surplus Disposal.

268.	STAHL, Michael. <u>Ethiopia: Political Contradictions in Agricultural Development</u>. Uppsala: Political Science As-
1974	sociation in Uppsala. [distr. by Raben & Sjoegren, Sweden and Africana Publishing Company, U.S.A.] 186 p.

Focuses on the social structure and political background of Ethiopian agriculture. Reviews post World War II Ethiopian land and agricultural policies until 1973. Concludes that the land and agricultural policies adopted by the Imperial Government enhanced a pattern of uneven development in the Southern provinces.

269.	STAM, Jerome M. "The Effects of Public Law 480 on Canadian Wheat Exports." <u>Journal of Farm Economics</u> 46 (4): 805-
1964	819, November.

Suggests that U.S. P.L. 480 wheat exports depressed total Canadian exports during the fiscal 1955-60 period. Delineates possible harmful effects suffered by Canada. Demonstrates that Canadian wheat exports were reduced, largely as a result of P.L. 480 activities, on a percentage basis in an 18 country group, and on a percentage and quantity basis in a 16 country group examined in this study.

270.	STANLEY, Robert G. <u>Food for Peace: Hope and Reality of U.S. Food Aid</u>. New York: Gordon and Breach. 355 p.
1973

Provides an historical analysis of United States food aid programs, primarily P.L. 480 (Food for Peace) "to unravel and clarify who does what, and why, in the name of P.L. 480;" and "to produce alternatives from the future and an answer to the question: how can we [United States] produce and distribute enough of the proper foods?" Discusses beneficial ways of using food aid for development instead of using it as a means of boosting political status or as military aid. The documentation on the use of P.L. 480 in India, Colombia and Israel is very interesting.

271.	STEPANEK, Joe. "Food for Development: A Food Aid Policy." In <u>Food Aid for Development</u>, pp. 119-130. Edited by Hartmut
1978	Schneider. Paris: Development Centre, OECD.

Explains the components of a development oriented food aid policy for developing countries. Concludes that the following concepts should guide food and agricultural policies:

1) market incentives for agricultural growth; 2) price ceiling and floors for foodgrain; 3) humanitarian uses of food; 4) food reserves in developing countries; and 5) a food management system emphasizing and implementing policies encouraging agricultural growth, employment expansion, the achievement of food self-reliance and the provision of food to the poor. Discusses other considerations and qualifications of food policy including: 1) implications of food policy for equitable growth; 2) public and private sector roles in food policy; 3) role of incentive prices for agricultural development; 4) frequency of public interventions to stabilize food prices; 5) publicly subsidized food ration systems; 6) public works programs; and 7) budgetary implications of varying food aid levels.

272. STEVENS, Christopher. "Food Aid: Good, Bad, or Indifferent? Evidence of Four African Case Studies." In Food Aid for Development pp. 50-59. Edited by Hartmut Schneider. Paris: Development Centre of the OECD.

1978

Describes the nature and scope of research work undertaken by the Overseas Development Institute (ODI) from 1976-1978 on the impact of food aid in four African countries: Botswana, Upper Volta, Lesotho and Tunisia. Analyzes the indirect impacts of food aid on the policies of the recipient governments. The four case studies illustrate the situation in countries at different levels of economic development from Upper Volta, the poorest, to Tunisia, the richest. The results indicate that conclusions drawn in most of the food aid literature (largely based on studies conducted in South Asia and Latin America) are generally not applicable to Africa. Contends that "as a country's level of economic development changes so do the ways in which it can use food aid effectively." Discusses food aid and agricultural production, maternal child health and supplemental feeding projects, food-for-work, and project vs. programme aid. Concludes that development food aid has not significantly disrupted agricultural production in the four countries because its supply has been limited. Nevertheless, harmful effects may occur if it is provided on a larger scale and used inappropriately.

273. STEVENS, Christopher. "Food Aid: More Sinned Against than Sinning?" ODI Review, No. 2: 71-85.

1977

Analyzes trade-offs between food aid and cash aid to developing countries. Compares and contrasts the harmful and beneficial effects of food aid based on data illuminating the impact of food aid in Botswana, Upper Volta and Lesotho concentrating on its developmental uses. Topics discussed include the effects of food aid on prices, production; consumption, nutrition, commercial imports, taste, and governmental policies. Suggests that the recipient government's ambivalence to keep food aid projects functioning may be "responsible for the failure of food aid to receive the credit which it is due."

274. STEVENS, Christopher. "Food Aid and Nutrition: the Case of Botswana." Food Policy 3 (1): 18-28, February.

1978

Describes the impact of food aid on the performance of primary school children and vulnerable groups, on the family economy, and on the government's recurrent budget. Draws connections between food aid and nutrition. Concludes that although food aid undoubtedly misses many of the poorest people, it has added to the recurrent resources for education and health.

275. STOKEY, Edith; and ZECKHAUSER, Richard. A Primer for Policy Analysis. New York: W. W. Norton & Company, Inc. 356 p.

1978

Comprehensive overview of the principles of policy analysis in the public sector. Although this work does not focus specifically on food policy, it provides the novice with an important introduction to the tools of the trade and to the structure common to all policy problems.

276. STRYKER, Richard. "The World Bank and Agricultural Development: Food Production and Rural Poverty." World Development, Volume 7: 325-336.

1979

Discussion of the core relationship between increasing food production and reducing rural poverty. The author claims that: "Concessionary transfers of food aid are unlikely to expand notably in coming years; the trend is in the opposite direction." Furthermore, the World Bank is not likely to provide ongoing agricultural assistance necessary to increase domestic foodstuffs production in the Third World. According to the author, "The Consultative Group for Food Production and Investment (CGFPI), organized by the Bank and FAO in response to demands from the 1974 World Food Conference for increased external investments, is virtually moribund already, an ephemeral symbolic gesture to the food crisis."

277. SVEDBERG, Peter. "The Price-Disincentive Effect of Food Aid Revisited: A Comment." Economic Development and Cultural Change 27 (3): 549-552, April.

1979

This critique of Paul I. Isenman and H. W. Singer's article, "Food Aid: Disincentive Effects and Their Policy Implications," (Economic Development and Cultural Change 25, No. 2, [January 1977]: 205-37) attempts to show that "disincentive effects of food aid are even less of problem than conceived of by Isenman and Singer."

278.

1979

TALBOT, Ross B. "The European Community's Food Aid Programme--An Integration of Ideology, Strategy, Technology and Surpluses." Food Policy 4 (4): 269 ff., November.

The author highlights the historical evolution of the European Economic Coummunity's food aid policy and programmes from 1957 to 1977 emphasizing the interactions between ideology, strategy, technology and food surpluses. He recounts EEC food aid issues such as the controversy between multilateral and bilateral food aid, food aid as a foreign policy instrument, food aid and forward planning and the Common Agricultural Policy (CAP). Predicts the favorable expansion of the European food aid program for developing countries.

279.

1977

TALBOT, Ross B. "The Three US Food Policies--An Ideological Interpretation." Food Policy 2 (1): 3-16, February.

Describes the conflict of three food ideologies vying for dominance in the area of American food policy. Ideologies are characterized as neo-Hamiltonianism (the market economy) neo-Jeffersonianism (the public economy) and neo-Madisonianism (the pluralist, interest-group economy). Discusses the impact of these ideologies on the formulation of the new food politics of the Carter Administration.

280.

1977

TALBOT, Ross B., editor. The World Food Problem and U.S. Food Politics and Policies: 1972-1976, A Reading Book. Amers, Iowa: Iowa State University Press. 381 p.

Book of readings on the world food problem and alternative solution. Of particular note are Chapter VIII, Food Aid and Development Assistance; Chapter XI, Instruments of Food Policy in the Making; and Chapter XII, The World Food Problem and U.S. Food Politics. These chapters provide lively discussion and debate between food experts on the role of food aid in developing countries and the requirements for the establishment of a coherent United States and international food policy.

281.   TALBOT, Ross B., editor. *The World Food Problem and U.S. Food Politics and Policies: 1978.* Ames, Iowa: The Iowa
1979   State University Press. 210 p.

Contains a variety of articles on topics ranging from a description of the world food situation in 1978 to building a United States food reserve. The section on "The National and International Politics of Food Aid" in Chapter Three is of particular interest and summarizes four articles: 1) "Food Aid: Beyond Deploring," by Mark Schomer; 2) "New Directions for U.S. Food Assistance," by the U.S.D.A. Special Task Force on the Operation of Public Law 480; and 3) "Changing Conditions in Egypt Ensure Role as Major U.S. Farm Market," by John B. Parker, Jr. World food policy developments are highlighted in Chapter II.

282.   TARRANT, John R. *Food Policies.* New York: John Wiley and Sons. 338 p.
1980

The interconnections between agriculture, employment, income distribution, malnutrition and development are discussed in relation to their impact on governmental food policy. Governmental food policy interventions affecting agricultural production, food consumption and food trade are examined in the developed market economies, the centrally planned economies and in developing countries. Chapter 7 provides an assessment of the impact of food aid on recipient countries including an analysis of the following factors: production and price effects, policy effects, budgetary and employment effects, debts and dependency, programme versus project food aid, the World Food Programme, P.L. 480, Supplemental Feeding, Food for Work Programmes, Emergency Aid and speed and dependability of food aid.

283.   TIMMER, C. P. "China's Food Policy Shifting Gears." *Human Ecology Forum* 6: 8-10, Spring.
1976

Brief discussion of China's food policy before and after the Cultural Revolution.

284.   TIMMER, C. Peter. "Fertilizer and Food Policy in LDCs." *Food Policy* 1 (2): 143-154, February.
1976

Using a simple macro-model, the relationships between fertilizer price increases, food production and rising food prices are shown. The food policy implications of these relationships are discussed. Places special emphasis on the impact of price because of its frequent use as a policy instrument.

285. TIMMER, C. Peter. "Food Policy in China." Food Research Institute Studies 15 (1): 53-69.

1976

Description of how China solved its food problem through two fundamental components: 1) increasing food supplies through agricultural growth; and 2) ensuring access to those supplies by means of socialist distribution mechanisms. Focuse's on small-scale rural industry as one major component of China's food policy and provides a broad sketch of the strategies and mechanisms used by the Chinese in their agricultural development effort.

286. TIMMER, C. Peter; FALCON, Walter P.; and NELSON, Gerald C. "China's Food Policy: Incentives and Mechanisms." Ceres 12 (2): 25-30, March-April.

1979

Discussion of the components of China's successful food policy focusing on agricultural incentives and production techniques. Contends that except for the unique aspect of employing surplus agricultural labor in rural factories rather than urban ones, the Chinese are increasing food production with physical techniques that are consistent with many economic models used in other developing nations. These food policies may be equally effective in other areas if the twin complements to the Chinese physical model are also implemented: 1) organizational and personal incentives; and 2) social and bureaucratic mechanisms of distribution which ensure equitable access to food supplies.

287. TOLLEY, George S.; and ZADROZNY, Peter A., editors. Trade, Agriculture, and Development. Cambridge, Mass.: Ballinger Publishing Co. 218 p.

1975

Provides an understanding of development in a context that encompasses both agriculture and trade. Chapter Two, "The Impact of U.S. Agricultural Policies on Trade of the Developing Countries," looks at the impact of less protective U.S. policies on less developed countries and compares the gains (or losses) to less developed countries for various raw and processed commodities. Other topics discussed are: the impact of price on rice trade in Asia; the interaction of growth strategy, agriculture and foreign trade in India; agricultural trade in the economic development of Taiwan; and growth, capital import and agriculture in Korea.

288. TOMA, Peter A. The Politics of Food for Peace: Executive-Legislative Interaction. Tuscon, Arizona: The University of Arizona Press. 195 p.

1967

Presents a detailed investigation of the reasons for "the 1964 swing in congressional attitudes away from expansion of the Food for Peace program." Congressional debate, voting patterns, and factors affecting the formulation of food aid policy are presented. Places emphasis on the politics involved in the passage of the 1964 food aid legislation and the shaping of domestic agricultural politics.

289.   TREZISE, Philip.   International Grain Reserves: Who Pays. Washington, D.C.: The Brookings Institution. 66 p.

1976

Arguing for the establish of multilaterally-held grain reserves to fulfill the separate objectives of famine relief and the stabilization of commercial markets, Trezise points out the dangers of unilaterally financed cereal stocks. He discusses appropriate food policy, considerations and major problems associated with the establishment of buffer stocks, i.e. the international allocation of costs, stock levels and the release of reserves to needy nations.

290.   TRURAN, James A.   "Brazil Fine-tuning Farm Policies to Fight Inflation, Expand Food Production."   Foreign Agri-

1979   culture 17 (20): 17-18, November.

Discussion of Brazilian agricultural policies under the administration of President Figueiredo. Describes specific food programs of the Brazilian Government.

291.   TRURAN, James A.   "U. S. Producers Watching Brazil's Wheat Autarky Policy Review." Foreign Agriculture 16 (40): 4-5,

1977   October 3.

Description of the pros and cons of Brazil's widely publicized wheat self-sufficiency program and agricultural policies affecting the wheat sector.

292.   TUOMI, Helena. "Food Import and Neo-colonialism." In The Political Economy of Food, pp. 1-22. Edited by Vilo Harle.

1978   Farnborough, Hants, England: Saxon House, Teakfield Lt.

Examines the reasons for global food dependence and its special economic, political and security function within the international system. Measures the degree and composition of the food dependence of underdeveloped countries as a percentage of food imports in production. Contends that food aid programmes "became a dumping measure in many cases, and the share of gifts or concessional sales has since been reduced and normal commercial sales have reduced and normal commercial sales have replaced them." Discusses food aid policies, issues of self-sufficiency and the impact of food imports on agricultural development in Latin America.

293.

1979

UNITED NATIONS. "Council Urges Highest Priority for Food and Agriculture in 1980's." U.N. Monthly Chronicles 16 (6): 47-50, July-October.

Report of the fifth ministerial session of the World Food Council including the Council's: 1) declaration that no right was more fundamental than the right to food and no goal more urgent than the goal of overcoming the hunger of a billion people; 2) recommendation that in order to reinforce the food priority, developing countries should consider establishing a high-level food management authority such as an Inter-ministerial Co-ordinating Committee to monitor policies for increasing the priority for food, and oversee reparation and implementation of food strategies; and 3) call for a New Food Aid Convention and a new International Wheat Agreement as key elements of world food security.

294.

1980

UNITED NATIONS. "Developed Countries Asked to Provide Greater Food Aid." U.N. Monthly Chronicles. 17 (1): 59, January.

Summary of U.N. General Assembly recommendations on food aid and development issues. Encourages: 1) developed countries and international institutions to provide at least $8.3 billion dollars of concessional food aid; 2) governments to support the international food aid convention for securing a minimum flow of 10 million tons of food aid, even in times of high prices and food shortage; 3) governments to increase their assistance for agricultural inputs; and 4) the International Monetary Fund and the World Bank to provide balance-of-payments support for meeting the food import bills of low-income, food-deficit countries.

295.

1979

UNITED NATIONS. "$375 Million Agriculture Fund Plan Approved." U.N. Monthly Chronicles. 16 (1): 50-1, January.

The U.N. Governing Council of the International Fund for Agricultural Development (IFAD) describes its $375 million commitments for projects in developing countries aimed at increasing food production and eliminating rural poverty.

296.   U. S. AGENCY FOR INTERNATIONAL DEVELOPMENT, Area Auditor General, West Africa. <u>Report on Public Law 480 Title I and</u>
1979   <u>Title II Programs in the People's Revolutionary Republic of Guinea</u>. Washington, D.C.: USAID. 9 p.

Examines the effectiveness of the Government of Guinea's management controls over P.L. 480 programs and reports on problem areas.

297.   U. S. CONGRESS. House. Committee on Agriculture. <u>Food Relief Programs</u>. 93rd Congress, 2nd session. 67 p.
1974

Discussion of various food relief programs including the donation of live beef cattle to Honduras and other nations experiencing massive food shortages; the provision of non-surplus agricultural commodities for humanitarian purposes; and the purchase of animals and animal food products for use in domestic and foreign food aid programs.

298.   U. S. CONGRESS. House. Committee on Agriculture, Subcommittee on Tobacco. <u>Suspension of Public Law 480 Barter</u>
1973   <u>Program for Tobacco</u>. 93rd Congress, 1st session. 85 p.

Examines USDA suspension of tobacco barter program and its effect on tobacco exports.

299.   U. S. CONGRESS. House. Committee on Appropriations. <u>Agriculture, Rural Development and Related Agencies Appropria-</u>
1978   <u>tions for 1979, Part 6</u>. 95th Congress, 2nd session. 867 p.

Reviews FY 79 appropriations for USDA, USAID and related agencies. Testimony of Kelly M. Harrison, US General Sales Manager and Dale I. Hathaway, USDA Assistant Secretary, provides a budget justification for P.L. 480 and CCC programs. Discusses modification of regulatory revisions permitting the CCC to finance agricultural sales to North Vietnam.

300.   U. S. CONGRESS. House. Committee on Appropriations. <u>Agriculture, Rural Development and Related Agencies Appropria-</u>
1980   <u>tions for 1981, Part 2: Agricultural Programs</u>. Hearing, February 22, 25-27, 29, 1980. 96th Congress, 2nd session. 892 p.

Contains USDA Fiscal Year 81 budget requests including: 1) justification for P.L. 480 agricultural commodity exports (p. 502-514); 2) description of P.L. 480 assistance planned for fiscal year 81; 3) listing of P.L. 480 concessional sales allocations by country for FY79 and FY80 (p. 437-38); and 4) a report on P.L. 480 voluntary agency and World Food Program operations (439-449).

301.

1979
U. S. CONGRESS. House. Committee on Appropriations. <u>Foreign Assistance and Related Programs Appropriations for 1980, Part 4.</u> 96th Congress, 1st Session. 1029 p.

Continuation of hearings on FY79 and FY80 budget requests. Focuses on AID programs. Contains testimony of several AID officials including Goler T. Butcher, AID Assistant Administrator for Africa, who describes the budget requests for Africa, including the Sahel Development Program; and John H. Sullivan, Assistant Administrator for Asia, who submits justifications for P.L. 480 assistance to Asia.

302.

1979
U. S. CONGRESS. House. Committee on Appropriations. <u>Foreign Assistance and Related Programs Appropriations for 1980, Part 5.</u> 96th Congress, 1st Session. 460 p.

Continuation of hearings on FY79 and FY80 budget requests. Contains testimony from public witnesses. Those pertinent to food aid or food policy are: 1) Tony Jackson, "Food Aid Versus the Peasant Farmer: The Case of Haiti," (p. 380-386); 2) George P. Potter, "PL 480 Foreign Assistance Food-Aid Dependency or Development?" (p. 369-379); 3) Frederick C. Cuny, "Food Donations After Disasters and in Relation to Agricultural Development" (p. 387-420); and 4) Jo Froman, "PL 480 Food Assistance in Guatemala" (p. 421-452).

303.

1975
U. S. CONGRESS. House. Committee on Foreign Affairs. <u>Conference Report on International Development and Food Assistance Act of 1975.</u> 94th Congress, 1st Session. 41 p.

Contains FY76 and transition quarter appropriations for foreign aid programs, including P.L. 480 and disaster relief food aid.

304.

1974
U. S. CONGRESS. House. Committee on Foreign Affairs. Subcommittee on Africa. <u>The Crisis of the African Drought.</u> 93rd Congress, 2nd Session. Washington, D.C.: Government Printing Office. 143 p.

Discusses the food aid needs of six West African countries of the Sahel; Mali, Mauritania, Chad, Upper Volta, Niger and Senegal. Highlights food and agricultural development problems of Ethiopia, Gambia, Nigeria, Sudan, Ghana, Central African Republic, Cameroon, Guinea, Ivory Coast,

Dahomey, Tanzania and Kenya. The appendix contains reprints of articles on the Sahelian drought crisis.

305.   U. S. CONGRESS. House. Committee on Foreign Affairs. <u>Economic Support Fund Programs in the Middle East</u>. 96th
1979   Congress, 1st Session. 79 p.

Report of a staff study mission to Egypt, Syria, Jordan, the West Bank, and Gaza, November 24 through December 15, 1978. Examines the impact of US aid programs, including PL 480 and makes recommendations for the future.

306.   U. S. CONGRESS. House. Committee on Foreign Affairs. <u>Food Security Act of 1980</u>. House Report, 96-966, 96th Congress,
1980   2nd Session. 27 p.

Recommends passage of the Food Security Act of 1980 (H.R. 6635), and calls for the establishment of a United States wheat reserve for meeting food needs in developing countries through stockpiling and designation of CCC stocks. The reserve would work in conjunction to P.L. 480 to extend the supply of wheat to food-deficit nations.

307.   U. S. CONGRESS. House. Committee on Foreign Affairs. <u>Foreign Assistance Legislation for FY80-FY81, Part 1</u>. Hear-
1979   ings, February 5-7, March 9, 14, 21. 96th Congress, 1st Session. 699 p.

Investigates various aspects of the Administration request for FY80 foreign economic and security assistance. Testimony of Bob Bergland, Secretary USDA, reviews the status of P.L. 480 food assistance program; discusses the administration of the program; and provides handy tables (p. 140-144) summarizing P.L. 480 activity by country.

308.   U. S. CONGRESS. House. Committee on Foreign Affairs. <u>Foreign Assistance Legislation for FY80-81, Part 6: Economic
1979   and Military Assistance Programs in Africa</u>. 96th Congress, 1st Session. 612 p.

Examines aid to African countries including information about progress and commitment data for Kenya under P L 480. Provides an explanation of P L 480 program administration by Goler T. Butcher, AID Assistant Administrator for Africa and an overview of the Sahel Regional Development Program by James Kelley, AID Director of the Office of SAHEL.

309.   U. S. CONGRESS. House. Committee on Foreign Affairs. Removing Prohibitions Relating to Uganda. House Report, 96-
1979   395. 96th Congress, 1st Session. 4 p.

Recommends repeal of prohibitions on the provision of international development and food assistance to Uganda.

310.   U. S. CONGRESS. House. Committee on Foreign Affairs and Committee on Agriculture. Food Security Act of 1979.
1979   Hearing, July 10. 96th Congress, 1st Session. 73 p.

Examines the merits of the Food Security Act of 1979 (H.R. 4489) and similar bills designed to establish a United States wheat reserve to complement P.L. 480 in times of limited supply. Includes testimony of Bob Bergland, Secretary of the USDA and Dale E. Hathaway, Under Secretary of USDA's International Affairs and Commodity Programs positing arguments against international wheat cartel formation.

311.   U. S. CONGRESS. House. Committee on Foreign Affairs, Subcommittee on Africa. The Drought Crisis in the African
1973   Sahel. 93rd Congress, 2nd Session. Washington, D.C.: Government Printing Office. 224 p.

Contains the testimony of Thomas A. Johnson, West Africa correspondent to the New York Times regarding the emergency food aid needs of the Sahelian countries. The appendix contains various background information and policy recommendation on the Sahel and Progress Reports Nos. 1-4 of the Food and Agriculture Organization of the United Nations, Office for the Sahelian Relief Operation.

312.   U. S. CONGRESS. House. Committee on Foreign Affairs, Subcommittee on International Resources, Food, and Energy.
1975   Food Problems of Developing Countries: Implications for U.S. Policy. 94th Congress, 1st Session. 355 p.

Overview of U. S. food production potential and U. S. food aid policy. Review of P.L. 480 programs and shipments by country, FY73-76. Description of emergency food aid relief program in Ethiopia; and a discussion of the role of voluntary agencies in international food and development assistance.

313.   U. S. CONGRESS. House. Document Room Superintendent. Agricultural Trade Development and Assistance Act of 1954
1976   and Amendments. 94th Congress, 1st Session. 66 p.

Contains text of P.L. 480 legislation and amendments from the 83rd through 94th Congress.

314.   U. S. CONGESS House. International Relations Committee. <u>Foreign Assistance Legislation for FY78. Part 3: Economic</u>
1977   <u>and Military Assistance Programs in Africa</u>. 95th Congress, 1st Session. 286 p.

Review of aid to African nations, including programs focusing on food production and AID food assistance to Africa under P.L. 480.

315.   U. S. CONGRESS. House. International Relations Committee. <u>Foreign Assistance Legislation for FY78, Part 8</u>. 95th
1977   Congress, 1st Session. 78 p.

Contains recommendations of U.S. voluntary agencies and private citizens suggesting improvements to the P.L. 480 program. Summarizes a subcommittee report on development assistance and food policy.

316.   U. S. CONGRESS. House. International Relations Committee. <u>Foreign Assistance Legislation for FY79, Part 1</u>. 95th
1978   Congress, 2nd Session. 564 p.

Assessment of the merits of the US food and development assistance programs including testimony from USAID and USDA officials, the Interreligious Task Force on U. S. Food Policy; Church World Service and Lutheran World Relief; OECD; and the Tokyo International Symposium. Highlights the need for continued P.L. 480 assistance.

317.   U. S. CONGRESS. House. International Relations Committee. <u>Foreign Assistance Legislation for FY79. Part 3: Economic</u>
1978   <u>and Military Assistance Programs in Africa</u>. 95th Congress, 2nd Session. 227 p.

Focusing on aid to African countries, this document provides an overview of AID's authorization request for FY79 Sahel region multi-donor development program and describes various food and agricultural assistance projects by type, sponsor, country and financing source.

318. U. S. CONGRESS. House. International Relations Committee. <u>Foreign Assistance Legislation for FY79. Part 5: Economic and Military Aid Programs in Europe and the Middle East.</u> 95th Congress, 2nd Session. 742 p.

1978

Contains testimony of Joseph C. Wheeler, AID Assistant Administrator, Bureau for Near East providing an overview of P.L. 480 projects in Egypt.

319. U. S. CONGRESS. House. International Relations Committee. Subcommittee on Asian and Pacific Affairs. <u>Foreign Assistance Legislation for FY79. Part 6: Economic and Security Assistance in Asia and the Pacific.</u> 95th Congress, 2nd Session. 334 p.

1978

Contains testimony of John H. Sullivan, AID Assistant Administrator for Asia providing an overview of FY79 authorization requests for P.L. 480 and other development assistance to Thailand, the Philippines, Indonesia, India, Bangladesh, Pakistan, Nepal, and Sri Lanka.

320. U. S. CONGRESS. House. International Relations Committee. <u>Foreign Assistance Legilsation for FY79. Part 8: Development Assistance and Public Law 480 Amendment.</u> 95th Congress, 2nd Session. 219 p.

1978

Examines various Foreign Assistance Act amendments designed to improve AID development programs and the administration of P.L. 480 programs abroad.

321. U. S. CONGRESS. House. International Relations Committee. <u>Implementation of Recommendations of the World Food Conference.</u> 94th Congress, 2nd Session. 77 p.

1976

AID report on food aid programs and technical assistance programs in keeping with the recommendations of the World Food Conference to improve developing countries food production systems and to minimize world hunger.

322. U. S. CONGRESS. House. International Relations Committee. <u>International Development and Food Assistance Act of 1977.</u> 95th Congress, 1st Session. 45 p.

1977

Conference report on the International Development and Food Assistance Act of 1977 which amended earlier P.L. 480 legislation. Presents budget and rationale for FY78 P.L. 480 authorization.

323.   U. S. CONGRESS. House. International Relations Committee.
        International Development and Food Assistance Act of 1978.
1978   House Report, 95-1545. 95th Congress, 2nd Session. 47 p.

Reviews the International Development and Food Assistance Act of 1978 (H.R. 12222) amending the Foreign Assistance Act of 1961 and authorizing P.L. 480 FY79 appropriations for international food and development assistance.

324.   U. S. CONGRESS. House. International Relations Committee.
        International Development and Food Assistance Act of 1978.
1978   House Report, 95-1087. 95th Congress, 2nd Session. 118 p.

Recommends passage of the International Development and Food Assistance Act of 1978 and authorizes the CCC to pay ocean freight charges for P.L. 480 shipments.

325.   U. S. CONGRESS. House. International Relations Committee.
        International Emergency Wheat Reserve. 95th Congress, 2nd
1978   Session. 193 p.

Reviews various legislation requiring the establishment of U.S. domestic reserves to be used for food-deficit countries.

326.   U. S. CONGRESS. House. International Relations Committee.
        International Emergency Wheat Reserve Act of 1978. House
1978   Report, 95-1564, Part 2. 95th Congress, 2nd Session. 23 p.

Recommends passage of International Emergency Wheat Reserve Act of 1978 which would allow the President to draw from the reserves when regular P.L. 480 supplies could not be furnished.

327.   U. S. CONGRESS. House. International Relations Committee.
        "New Directions" Aid Programs in Asia: Indochina Refugees
1978   in Thailand. 95th Congress, 2nd Session. 75 p.

Report by Lewis Gulick and other members of a staff study mission to Thailand, Bangladesh, India, and Pakistan, in November-December 1977. Analyzes US aid programs, including P.L. 480, in light of the congressional mandate requiring foreign assistance to be channelled to the poor and to benefit the development policies and economic problems of the recipient.

328.   U. S. CONGRESS. House. International Relations Committee. New Directions in Development Aid Excerpts from the Legislation (As of January 1977). 95th Congress, 1st Session. 20 p.

1977

Reviews legislation enacted since 1973 which encouraged U. S. bilateral assistance programs to concentrate aid on agriculture, population planning and education projects. Particular attention is focused on the economic development benefits of P.L. 480 in developing nations.

329.   U. S. CONGRESS. House. International Relations Committee. Proposal for a Program in Appropriate Technology. 94th Congress, 2nd Session. 323 p.

1976

Examines proposals encouraging the development and dissemination of intermediate technologies for developing countries, including the 1975 provisions of the International Development and Food Assistance Act calling for technological assistance to developing countries.

330.   U. S. CONGRESS. House. International Relations Committee, Subcommittee on International Resources, Food and Energy. U. S. International Grain Policy: Sales and Management. 94th Congress, 1st Session. 34 p.

1975

Examines U.S. international grain policy emphasizing sales and management practices.

331.   U. S. CONGRESS. House Subcommittee on International Resources, Food and Energy of the Committee on International Relations. Food Problems of Developing Countries: Implications for U.S. Policy. Washington, D.C.: U.S. Government Printing Office. 355 p.

1975

Reports of leading government officials, agencies and technicians on international food problems. Discusses the need for a comprehensive assessment of U.S. food aid policy and the role of American agricultural technicians in developing countries.

332.   U. S. CONGRESS. House and Senate. International Development and Food Assistance Act of 1978: Public Law 95-424, in U. S. Code Congressional and Administrative News: P.L. 95-405 to 95-454. 95th Congress: 2nd Session. Washington, D.C.: West Publishing Company, November.

1978

"An Act to amend the Foreign Assistance Act of 1961 to

authorize development and economic assistance programs for fiscal year 1979, to make certain changes in the authorrities of that Act and the Agricultural Trade Development and Assistance Act of 1954, to improve the coordination and administration of United States development-related policies and programs, and for other purposes."

333.   U. S. CONGRESS. Public Law 95-501. Agricultural Trade Act of 1978. 95th Congress, 2nd Session. 8 p.

1978

Amends the Agricultural Act of 1954 to: 1) establish Agricultural Trade Offices in developing countries; 2) upgrade the title of Agricultural Attaches to Agricultural Counselor; 3) provide for an Under Secretary for International Affairs and Commodity Programs with the USDA; and 4) amend P.L. 480 to allow CCC financing of agricultural sales to the People's Republic of China.

334.   U. S. CONGRESS. House. Subcommittee on Foreign Agricultural Policy. Food for Peace, 1954-1978: Major Changes in Legislation. 96th Congress, 1st Session. 59 p.

1979

Summarizes the historical development and legislative evolution of the P.L. 480 program. Contains the relevant texts of the Agricultural Trade Development and Assistance Act of 1954 and its major amendments. Explains the underlying conditions for each major change in the legislation, including the Amendments to Public Law 480 in 1959 and 1964, the Food for Peace Act of 1966, Amendments to Food for Peace in 1968, changes in program emphasis, 1972-74, and the International Development and Food Assistance Acts of 1975 and 1977. Provides tables on major recipients of P.L. 480 aid, 1970-79, and agricultural commodities exported under P.L. 480 and government programs, FY55-75.

335.   U. S. CONGRESS. Senate. Committee on Agriculture, Nutrition and Forestry. Agricultural Trade Suspension Adjustment Act of 1980. 96th Congress, 2nd Session. 37 p.

1980

To lessen the adverse farm market effects of US suspension of agricultural exports to the Soviet Union, this report calls for: 1) the establishment of a five-year CCC wheat reserve to provide emergency P.L. 480 assistance to developing countries; 2) the passage of the Agricultural Trade Suspension Act of 1980; 3) the authorization of USDA longterm price support loans under the farm-held reserve program on the 1979-81 crops of wheat and feed grains.

336. U. S. CONGRESS. Senate. Committee on Agriculture, Nutrition and Forestry. <u>American Foreign Food Assistance: Public Law 480 and Related Materials</u>. 94th Congress, 2nd Session. 43 p.

1976

Summarizes the history of the Food for Peace Program. Contains statistical data on P.L. 480 food shipments and program costs.

337. U. S. CONGRESS. Senate. Committee on Agriculture, Nutrition and Forestry. <u>Food and Agriculture Act of 1977</u>. 95th Congress, 1st Session. 431 p.

1977

Recommends passage of the Food and Agriculture Act of 1977 with specific amendments; makes changes in the P.L. 480 program; and establishes a program for grain reserves.

338. U. S. CONGRESS. Senate. Committee on Agriculture, Nutrition and Forestry. <u>Implementation of World Food Conference Recommendations</u>. 94th Congress, 1st Session. 128 p.

1975

Reviews U. S. participation in World Food Council and UN Food and Agriculture Organization efforts to implement the recommendations of the World Food Conference from 1974 through 1975.

339. U. S. CONGRESS. Senate. Committee on Agriculture, Nutrition, and Forestry. <u>International Development and Food Assistance Act of 1975</u>. 94th Congress, 1st Session. 90 p.

1975

Summarizes the International Development and Food Assistance Act of 1975. Recommends its passage and includes provisions on implementation of World Food Conference recommendations, commodities resale by recipient countries and congressional-executive consultation on agricultural commodities negotiations.

340. U. S. CONGRESS. Senate. Committee on Agriculture, Nutrition and Forestry. <u>International Emergency Food Fund, and Amendments to the Price Support Program for Sugar</u>. Senate Report, 95-1151. 95th Congress, 2nd Session. 20 p.

1978

Recommends passage of a bill, the International Emergency Food Fund Act of 1978, to provide contingency USDA authority to purchase CCC stocks for famine relief and emergency food aid assistance to Third World nations.

341.   U. S. CONGRESS. Senate. Committee on Agriculture, Nutrition, and Forestry. <u>New Directions for U. S. Food Assistance: A Report of the Special Task Force on the Operation of Public Law 480.</u> 95th Congress, 2nd Session. 128 p.

1978

Examines the operations and organizational arrangements of the P.L. 480 program to determine the effectiveness of the program's administration. Topics discussed include; the formulation of US food aid policy; an assessment of food aid needs of developing countries; the establishment of future US food aid levels; tradeoffs between food aid and financial assistance; international cooperation on food security; absorptive capacity of the food aid recipient; the impact of food aid on the recipient's balance of payments; and the foreign policy results of US food aid. A major recommendation of the task force is that priority in U.S. bilateral food aid be placed on projects which promote economic development in countries experiencing shortfalls in food production or temporary balance-of-payments problems in time of worldwide shortages and high prices. They suggest that U.S. food aid policy be designated to promote secular employment growth for the unemployed and underemployed, because the "resulting new income streams will shift income distribution toward lower income groups which demand relatively greater quantities of food for consumption. The stronger demand for food provides increased incentives for domestic food production and places greater pressure on the recipient government to give renewed attention to increasing the productivity of its own agricultural sector."

342.   U. S. CONGRESS. Senate. Committee on Agriculture, Nutrition, and Forestry. <u>Selected Material Relating to P.L. 480.</u> 94th Congress, 1st Session. 33 p.

1975

Review of P.L. 480 provisions and legislative history.

343.   U. S. CONGRESS. Senate. Committee on Agriculture, Nutrition and Forestry. <u>World Food Security.</u> 93rd Congress, 1st Session. 104 p.

1973

Reviews history of world food relief programs, particularly the World Food Program and P.L. 480. Examines proposals for a strategic food reserve.

344. U. S. CONGRESS. Senate. Committee on Agriculture, Nutrition, and Forestry, Subcommittee on Agricultural Production, Marketing, and Stabilization of Prices and the Subcommittee on Foreign Agricultural Policy. <u>U. S. Food Stabilization and Foreign Commercial and Food Aid Demands</u>. 93rd Congress, 2nd Session. 179 p.

1974

Reviews U.S. policies affecting the supply of food grains to meet domestic and foreign demands. Discusses market development programs of P.L. 480.

345. U. S. CONGRESS. Senate. Committee on Agriculture, Nutrition and Forestry, Subcommittee on Foreign Agricultural Policy. <u>Foreign Food Assistance</u>. 93rd Congress, 2nd Session. 111 p.

1974

Examines the adequacy of P.L. 480 food aid programs and possible misuse of commodities designed to relieve hunger. Focuses on the cases of Vietnam and Cambodia where food aid may have been diverted for military purposes.

346. U. S. CONGRESS. Senate. Committee on Agriculture, Nutrition, and Forestry, Subcommittee on Foreign Agricultural Policy. <u>Foreign Food Assistance and Agricultural Development</u>. 94th Congress, 1st Session. 106 p.

1975

Makes recommendations on the favorable use of U. S. food aid in international development programs.

347. U. S. CONGRESS. Senate. Committee on Agriculture, Nutrition and Forestry, Subcommittee on Foreign Agricultural Policy. <u>Future of Food Aid</u>. 95th Congress, 1st Session. 137 p.

1977

Assesses P.L. 480 program management and countries. Discusses the impact of P.L. 480 on underdeveloped countries with respect to U.S. foreign policy, market development and humanitarian objectives. Projects the future of P.L. 480 multiannual grain agreements and reviews procedures assuring Title I proceeds are used for economic development.

348. U. S. CONGRESS. Senate. Committee on Agriculture, Nutrition, and Forestry, Subcommittee on Foreign Agricultural Policy. <u>Public Law 480 Aid for Refugees</u>. 96th Congress, 2nd Session. Washington, D.C.: GPO 29 p.

1980

Reviews United States use of food aid to meet refugee and emergency needs throughout the world, particularly in

Kampuchea, Pakistan, Afgahanistan and Somalia. Places emphasis on the use and effectiveness of P.L. 480 Title II food aid. Provides testimony of Victor Palmieri, Ambassador at Large and Coordinator for Refugee Affairs of the Department of State; Mrs. Kathleen Bittermann, Coordinator Food for Peace Office, Agency for International Development; and Fred Welz, Assistant General Manager and Assistant Administrator of the Foreign Agricultural Service, USDA.

349. U. S. CONGRESS. Senate. Committee on Agriculture, Nutrition and Forestry, Subcommittee on Foreign Agricultural Policy. <u>World Food Conference: Selected Materials for the Use of the U. S. Congressional Delegation to the World Food Conference.</u> 93rd Congress, 1st Session. 377 p.

1974

Contains background information on the world food crisis and U. S. food aid programs. Discusses measures for increasing food production in developing countries; policies for improving world food security; and provisions of the P.L. 480 program which foster self-help.

350. U. S. CONGRESS. Senate. Committee on Appropriations. <u>Agriculture and Related Agencies Appropriations, FY78. Part 1: Justifications.</u> 95th Congress, 1st Session. 1278 p.

1977

Pages 999 to 1009 contain budget justifications for FY78 P.L. 480 Programs.

351. U. S. CONGRESS. Senate. Committee on Appropriations. <u>Agriculture, Rural Development and Related Agencies Appropriations, FY79, Part 1: Justifications.</u> 96th Congress, 2nd Session. 1306 p.

1978

Pages 505-516 contain budget justification materials for P.L. 480.

352. U. S. CONGRESS. Senate. Committee on Finance. <u>Foreign Indebtedness to the U.S.</u> 93rd Congress, 1st Session. 62 p.

1973

Compilation of U.S. loans and grants made to foreign countries since 1917 and amounts of foreign indebtedness as of June 30, 1972. Includes data on P.L. 480 loans as of June, 1973.

353. U. S. CONGRESS. Senate. Committee on Foreign Relations. <u>Foreign Assistance Act of 1961.</u> Senate Report, 96-367.
1979   96th Congress, 1st Session. 14 p.

Recommends congressional authorization of funds for AID relief and rehabilitation assistance to hurricane victims in the Dominican Republic and Dominica, including P.L. 480 assistance.

354. U. S. CONGRESS. Senate. Committee on Foreign Relations, Subcommittee on South Asian Affairs and the Subcommittee
1973   on African Affairs. <u>World Food Grain Situation.</u> 93rd Congress, 1st Session. 94 p.

Discusses the world food problem in light of the U.S. role in providing food assistance for emergencies. Emphasizes the food crises in Bangladesh, the Sahel, and Pakistan. Reviews P.L. 480 and FAO food aid programs in these areas.

355. U. S. CONGRESS. Senate. Judiciary Committee. <u>World Hunger, Health, and Refugee Problems. Part 6: Mission to Africa,</u>
1975   <u>Asia, and the Middle East.</u> 94th Congress, 1st Session. 617 p.

Contains broad discussion on the relationship between health, world hunger and famine relief operations. The appendix contains many useful short articles on U.S. food policy and international aid programs.

356. U. S. CONGRESS. Senate. Judiciary Committee. Subcommittee on Refugees and Escapees and the Labor and Public Welfare
1973   Committee Subcommittee on Health. <u>World Hunger, Health, and Refugee Problems. Part 3: Development and Food Needs.</u> 93rd Congress, 1st Session. 152 p.

Focuses on the impact of food scarcities on developing countries; the importance of small farm productivity; and the U.S. role in international food aid programming.

357. U. S. CONGRESS. Senate. Select Committee on Nutrition and Human Needs. <u>U. S. Participation in the Food and Agri-</u>
1976   <u>culture Organization of the United Nations.</u> 94th Congress, 2nd Session. 134 p.

Review of U.S. participation in the FAO. Makes recommendations for coordinated multilateral food assistance program.

358. U. S. CONGRESS. Senate. Subcommittee on Foreign Agricultural Policy. <u>Amendments to the Agricultural Trade Development and Assistance Act of 1954.</u> Hearing, May 8. 96th Congress, 2nd Session. 96 p.

1979

Includes the full text of two bills, the Self-Reliant Development and International Food Assistance Reform Act of 1979 (S. 962) and the Food Assistance Reform Act of 1979 (S. 1053) which attempt to strengthen the impact of P.L. 480 on the local food production and market development of recipient countries. Both bills encourage the use of U. S. bilateral assistance to support economic development abroad; however, S. 1053 additionally calls for the cooperation and assistance of private enterprise and designates USDA as the administrator of P.L. 480 Title III. Includes testimony from Kelly M. Harrison, General Sales Manager, USDA; Kathleen S. Bitterman, USAID coordinator, Office of Food for Peace; Larry Minear, Development Policy Representative of Church World Service and Lutheran World Relief; Mark Schomer, Issue Analyst, Bread for the World; Stephen J. Gabbert, Executive Vice President, Rice Millers' Association; and S. A. Gregory, International Inc. Witnesses debate the issue of administrative control of Title III programs and the pros and cons of private agribusiness development aid over government assistance.

359. U. S. CONGRESS. Senate. Subcommittee on Foreign Agricultural Policy. <u>Export Promotion.</u> 95th Congress, 2nd Session. 235 p.

1978

Considers a bill, the Agricultural Trade Expansion Act of 1977, which would amend P.L. 480 to expand Commodity Credit Corporation credit financing programs for export and sale of agricultural commodities, and to allow nonmarket economy countries to participate in the program.

360. U. S. CONGRESS. Senate. Subcommittee on Foreign Agricultural Policy. <u>Food Aid to Cambodia.</u> 96th Congress, 1st Session. 25 p.

1979

Investigates US and international efforts to provide food aid for Kampuchean population and refugess. Ms. Kathleen Bittermann, Coordinator, AID Office of Food for Peace, provides specific information about the Kampuchean government's P.L. 480 emergency disaster food aid requests for fiscal year 1980.

361.   U. S. CONGRESS, Senate. Subcommittee on Foreign Agricultural Policy. <u>Implementation of the Agricultural Export Trade Expansion Act of 1978</u>. 96th Congress, 1st Session. 57 p.

1979

Recommends that USDA establish Agricultural Trade Offices abroad to promote agricultural exports, and that the US State Department upgrade its Agricultural Attaches to Agricultural Counselors. Discusses the role of the latter with respect to agricultural trade, P. L. 480 food assistance programs and CCC programs.

362.   U. S. CONGRESS. Senate. Subcommittee on Foreign Agricultural Policy. <u>International Food Reserves</u>. 95th Congress, 2nd Session. 70 p.

1978

Examines various proposals to create international emergency reserves, including: 1) the International Emergency Food Reserve Act of 1977 which links development of U.S. reserves to an international system of food reserves for humanitarian relief; 2) an amendment to the Agricultural Trade Development and Assistance Act of 1954 establishing an international grain reserve to assure adequate supplies for P.L. 480 aid; and 3) the International Wheat Reserve Act of 1978, establishing an international emergency wheat reserve under a new International Wheat Agreement.

363.   U.S.D.A.   <u>Annual Report on Public Law 480, Food for Peace, 1976/TQ</u>. Washington, D.C.: GPO 146 p.

1978

Highlights P.L. 480 acitivty during fiscal year 1976 (from July 1 through June 30) and the Transitional Quarter (TQ- from July 1 through September 30, 1976). The TQ was made effective in 1976 with the change of the United States' fiscal year from July 1 through June 30, to October 1 through September 30. Values fiscal year 1976 exports of agricultural commodities under P.L. 480 at $963.5 million, a decrease of $136.5 million from the previous year. Describes food aid programming of Title I and Title II to underdeveloped countries. Includes discussions on the use of foreign currencies; Title I legislative actions and balance of payments supports; Food for Work; U.S. contribution to the World Food Program; and the U.S. perspective on the Food Aid Convention of the International Wheat Agreement. Describes self-help projects in Tunisia, Ethiopia, Tanzania, Guinea, Afghanistan, Bangladesh, Korea, Indonesia, India, Sri Lanka, Pakistan, Portugal, Chili, Haiti, Jamaica, Egypt, Jordan, Israel and Syria. Contains over 75 pages of statistical tables on various aspects of P.L. 480.

364. U.S.D.A. "Bergland Cites U. S. World Food Policy." <u>Foreign Agriculture</u> 15 (26): 10, June 27.

1977

Excerpts from Secretary of Agriculture Bob Bergland in his June 20 address before the Third Ministerial Session of the World Food Council in Manila. The Secretary called for a reserve stock designed to reduce wide fluctuations in market prices, a sharing of reserve stock costs, and an end to interruptions in grain trade. He said food aid and development assistance must also play an important role in helping nations meet basic food requirements.

365. U.S.D.A. "Chile First to Buy U.S. Beef Under P.L. 480." <u>Foreign Agriculture</u> 2 (28): 11, July 13.

1964

Describes the terms of the first sale of U.S. beef under a P.L. 480 longterm credit agreement with Chile.

366. U.S.D.A. "EC Increases NFDM Food Aid." <u>Foreign Agriculture</u> 16 (26): 9, June 26.

1978

Short summary of EC plans to donate 150,000 metric tons of non-fat dry milk (NFDM) and 45,000 tons of butter in food aid during 1978. Major recipients include India, Bangladesh, Egypt, Pakistan, Vietnam and several major relief agencies.

367. U.S.D.A. "FY 1965 Figures for P.L. 480 Show Greater Use of Title IV--Now 24 Percent of All Agreements." <u>Foreign Agriculture</u> 3 (41): 9, October 11.

1965

Reviews growth of Title IV P.L. 480 agreements from 1962-65 including private trade agreements.

368. U.S.D.A. "Food for Freedom Program Extended for Two More Years." <u>Foreign Agriculture</u> 6 (37): 11, September, 9.

1968

Reviews 1968 amendments to the P.L. 480 food aid program with the primary aim of improving the U.S. balance-of-payments position. Gives special attention to the "Purcell Amendment" which makes it mandatory rather than discretionary for the U.S. Government to require that countries purchasing P.L. 480 commodities on long-term credit make advance payments upon delivery in dollars or local currency.

369.   U.S.D.A.   Food for Peace: Fiscal Year 1975.   Washington
       D.C.: GPO. 120 p.
1977

       Values fiscal year 1975 exports of agricultural commodities
       under Public Law 480 at approximately $1.1 billion, an in-
       crease of about $240 million over the previous year's total
       of $760 million. Major Title I food aid recipients were
       India, Egypt and Pakistan. Reviews food aid self-help pro-
       jects in Chile, Guinea, Egypt, Israel, Jordan, India and
       Korea; legislative requirements in food aid agreements; use
       and administration of foreign currencies; and mechanics of
       Food for Work and Emergency and Refugee Feeding programs.
       Includes 54 pages of statistical tables on various aspects
       of P.L. 480 aid to underdeveloped nations.

370.   U.S.D.A.   "Food for Peace Moves $11.4 Billion in Farm Pro-
       ducts." Foreign Agriculture 2 (29): 4-5, July 20.
1964

       Presents charts illustrating the value of commodities pro-
       grammed under Title I, P.L. 480 agreements signed 7/1/54
       through 12/31/63; P.L. 480 shipments to World Regions; and
       P.L. shipments by program type.

371.   U.S.D.A.   Food for Peace: 1977 Annual Report on Public Law
       480. Washington, D.C.: GPO. 91 p.
1978

       Highlight and summary of P.L. 480 activities from October
       1, 1976, through September 30, 1977. Focuses on promoting
       economic and community development within poor countries.
       Values fiscal year 1977, exports of agricultural commodi-
       ties under Public Law 480 at about $1,224.1 million, an
       increase of $260.6 million over the 12-month 1976 fiscal
       year and $222.9 million less than the 15 month period end-
       ing September 30, 1976. Describes self-help projects in
       Tunisia, Zambia, Morocco, Tanzania, Guinea, Pakistan, Indo-
       nesia, Philippines, Bangladesh, Egypt and Haiti. Among the
       chief recipients of concessional food aid were Egypt, Indo-
       nesia, Korea, Portugal, and Bangladesh. Includes 40 pages
       of statistical data on various aspects of P.L. 480.

372.   U.S.D.A.   Food for Peace: 1978 Annual Report on Public Law
       480. Washington, D.C.: GPO. 90 p.
1979

       Covers P.L. 480 activity from October 1, 1977, through
       September 30, 1978. Places emphasis on the use of food aid
       for development, particularly the new Food for Development
       (Title III) programs. The first Food for Development pro-
       grams were signed during the year--one with Bolivia and the
       other with Bangladesh. Values Public Law 480 exports during

the period at $1,062.5 million compared to $1,124.1 million in fiscal year 1977--a decrease of 6 percent. Describes 1978 P.L. 480 amendments. Chief recipients were Egypt, Indonesia, Bangladesh, Korea, and Pakistan. Discusses the International Emergency Food Reserve and the Food Aid Convention of the International Wheat Agreement. Describes self-help programs in the Dominican Republic, Lebanon, Bangladesh, Pakistan, India, and Sierra Leone. Contains 39 pages of statistical information on P.L. 480 aid to underdeveloped countries.

373. U.S.D.A. "Grain Self-Sufficiency by 1980? Czech Hopes Dim." *Foreign Agriculture* 15 (22): 7 May.

1977

Discusses agricultural conditions in Czechoslovakia focusing on grain imports. Points out that poor wheat production and drought precludes Czechoslovakia's chances of grain self-sufficiency in the 80's.

374. U.S.D.A. "Implications for the United States of Soviet 5-Year Plan." *Foreign Agriculture* 19 (25): 7, 16, June 21.

1976

Discusses Soviet agricultural policies in relation to U.S. markets. Suggests that given the policies contained in the 1976-80 Soviet Plan and the situation surrounding grain production in the USSR, "it is likely that the Soviet Union will remain a substantial market for U.S. grains for some years."

375. U.S.D.A. "Important New Direction Given U.S. Food Assistance." *Foreign Agriculture* 4 (49): 4-6, December 5.

1966

Describes the mechanics of the 1967-68 U.S. food aid program and compares it to P.L. 480 legislation prior to 1966. Key differences discussed include: 1) changes in the provisions under each title; 2) changes in the size and composition of the food aid program; 3) emphasis placed on self-help efforts; 4) removal of "surplus" requirement; 5) transition to dollar sales; 6) use of foreign currencies to support family planning projects; and 7) extension of U.S. market development programs.

376. USDA. "Initial FY 1978 Title 1, P.L. 480, Allocations Announced." *Foreign Agriculture* 15 (46): 16, November 14.

1977

Listing of USDA initial commodity and country allocations for fiscal 1978 under Title I of Public Law 480 which met the requirement that not less than 75 percent of food aid commodities be allocated to friendly countries meeting the International Development Association poverty criterion.

377. U.S.D.A. "New Directions in P.L. 480 Program Emphasized." <u>Foreign Agriculture</u>, 15 (43): 10, October.

1977

Short summary of the use of food aid as an effective market development tool. Describes new programs which will help P.L. 480 increase commercial agricultural sales such as: 1) a credit program to bridge the gap between the present 1- to 3-year CCC export credit sales program and the 20- to 40-year loans extended under Title 1 of Public Law 480; and 2) a non-commercial risk assurance program "to assure the export seller that payment will be received from the commodity credit corporation should a draft be dishonored as the result of a non-commercial risk occurence."

378. U.S.D.A. "President Notes Achievements of Food for Peace Program." <u>Foreign Agriculture</u> 3 (15): 20, April 12.

1965

U. S. exports of farm products under P.L. 480 hit $1.7 billion in 1964 and benefited not only millions of people overseas but the United States as well. President Lyndon B. Johnson chronicles these achievements in a March 31 message to the Congress.

379. U.S.D.A. "President Proposes Consortium Approach to India Food Aid." <u>Foreign Agriculture</u> 5 (8): 3-5, 11, February 20.

1967

Excerpts from President Lyndon B. Johnson's February 2nd address to Congress on Indian food aid. The President points out "the level of food aid will decline as self-help measures take hold, until that point is reached, food aid is an inescapable duty of the world community." He proposes an India Aid Consortium organized under the chairmanship of the World Bank which would make food aid part of a multilateral assistance program and integrate food aid with broader programs of economic assistance. Summarizes U.S. food aid policy in India.

380. U.S.D.A. "P.L. 480: A Backgrounder on Food for Peace." <u>Foreign Agriculture</u>, 17 (19): 25-26, October.

1979

Updates the basic operational mechanisms of Title I, Title II and Title III of P.L. 480.

-97-

381.   U.S.D.A.   "Public Law 480 Approaches Its 15th Birthday."
       Foreign Agriculture 7 (20): 3-7, May 16.
1969
       Historical review of the U.S. Public Law 480 food aid program and its evolution from a surplus disposal program to one emphasizing economic development. Describes the successful transition from foreign currency sales to sales for dollars under Title I and the mechanics of negotiating a P.L. 480 Title I agreement. Enumerates benefits of the food aid program including: 1) the removal of price-depressing surpluses of the American farmer allowing him more opportunity to produce and greater income; 2) the expansion of American agricultural export outlets; 3) the improvement of the U.S. balance of payments position by saving dollars that may otherwise be spent overseas; and 4) the employment of more U.S. enterprises whose functions support the production, storage, processing, and transportation of farm products.

382.   U.S.D.A.   "P.L. 480--Funded Research Includes Studies on Ecology and Pollution." Foreign Agriculture 8 (43): 10,
1970   October, 26.

       Describes projects funded by Public Law 480 research grants in India, Poland and Finland.

383.   U.S.D.A. "Public Law 480 is Cited as Important to Economic Growth of India and Israel." Foreign Agriculture 2 (11):
1964   5-6, March 16.

       Documents the statements of Indian and Israeli government officials praising the benefits of the P.L. 480 program at a meeting of the FAO-UN Consultative Group on Surplus Disposal.

384.   U.S.D.A.   "P.L. 480 Pace Picks Up During March and April."
       Foreign Agriculture 9 (19): 16, May 10.
1971
       Description and dollar value of 13 new country-to-country P.L. 480 Title I agreements and one private trade entity agreement to Cambodia, India, Guinea, Tunisia, Indonesia, Paraguay, Pakistan, Afghanistan, Vietnam, Dominican Republic, Korea, Philippines and Sierra Leone.

385.   U.S.D.A. "P.L. 480 Programs Gain Dollar Sales as Soft Currency Sales Decline." Foreign Agriculture 9 (33): 6-7,
1971   August 16.

In a four year period from fiscal year 1967 to 1970, P.L. 480 dollar sales rose from $194 million to $436 million and foreign currency sales dropped from $736 million to $267 million. Based on the 1970 Annual Report on P.L. 480, this report explains U.S. food aid policy responsible for the shift. Describes Title II activities and two new types of P.L. 480 market promotion programs.

386. U.S.D.A. "P. L. 480 Sales Total $284 Million in May-September." Foreign Agriculture 9 (43): 16, October 25.

1971

Lists agreements under P.L. 480 signed during this period. Describes specific recipient projects of Pakistan, South Vietnam, Morocco, India, Colombia, Iran, Guinea, Ecuador, Israel, Indonesia, Afghanistan, Lebanon and Cambodia.

387. U.S.D.A. "Said President Johnson upon Signing the New Food Aid Legislation--'The Only Long-term Solution is Self-help." Foreign Agriculture 4 (49): 3, December 5.

1966

Excerpts from Presdient Lyndon B. Johnson's speech upon authorizing the Food for Freedom (continuation of P.L. 480) program including a statement of opposition to a provision in the bill precluding food aid to countries that sell, furnish or permit their ships or aircraft to transport any equipment, materials or commodities to either North Vietnam or Cuba.

388. U.S.D.A. "Spanish Farm Co-op Federation Signs P.L. 480 Agreement for $35 Million of U.S. Feed Grains." Foreign Agriculture 3 (38): 9, September 20.

1965

Describes the mechanics of a $35-million Title IV Public Law 480 private trade agreement allowing a Spanish federation of agricultural cooperatives to buy 600,000 metric tons of U.S. feed grains over a 3 year period.

389. U.S.D.A. "Title I Food for Peace Shipments Near $900 Million Last Year." Foreign Agriculture 4 (29): 10, July 18.

1966

Summary of Food for Peace (P.L. 480) activity in 1965. Delineates CCC costs, ocean transportation costs, volume of commodities shipped, and number of Title I agreements.

390. U.S.D.A. "Two-Way Benefits of Food for Peace Are Cited as P.L. 480 is Extended for 2 More Years." Foreign Agriculture, 2 (42): October 19.

1964

Highlights benefits of P.L. 480 program on the eve of the renewal of the program from 1964-1966. Discusses the role of P.L. 480 in sales promotion in 67 countries, in supporting trade and in building new commercial customers. Lists twenty-three changes in P.L. 480 legislation.

391. U.S.D.A. "U. S. Beef Eligible for Export Under P.L. 480." Foreign Agriculture 2 (26): 11, June 29.

1964

Announcement of the inclusion of U.S. beef in Public Law 480 food aid programs. The announcement stressed the U.S. intention to export beef under P.L. 480 in a way that is not detrimental to established commercial trading relations.

392. U.S.D.A. "U. S. Food-Aid Share Dips, But is Still No. 1," by Susan A Libbin. Foreign Agriculture, 15 (43): 9-11, October.

1977

Summarizes 1977 changes in food aid legislation and explains the sharp 1975 food aid reductions. Suggests that "As developing countries have expanded economic growth and foreign exchange reserves, they have tended to increase commercial purchases from the United States, and reduce or even terminate their need for food aid."

393. U.S.D.A. "U. S. Goals in World Food Policy." Foreign Agriculture, 17 (19): 2, October.

1979

Remarks by Secretary of Agriculture Bob Bergland to the World Food Council in September 1979 urging: 1) technical assistance for the development of the agricultural sectors of poor countries; 2) support for a new International Wheat Agreement and Food Aid Convention; and 3) establishment of food security systems in the developing countries.

394. U.S.D.A. "U.S. Grain Reserves, Crop Set-Asides Announced." Foreign Agriculture 15 (37): 5-6, September, 12.

1977

Describes United States plans to establish additional strategic grain reserves including: 1) a comprehensive plan to place 30-35 million metric tons of food and feed grains in reserve prior to the beginning of the 1978/79 marketing year; 2) the Administration's intentions to implement a 20 percent set-aside on 1978-crop wheat; and 3) an immediate increase in the loan rates for 1977 crop feedgrains.

395.   U.S.D.A.   "Vitamin-fortified U. S. Nonfat Dry Milk Bought
       for Distribution in Overseas Donation Program." Foreign
1965   Agriculture 3 (23): 8, June 7.

       Description of the incorporation of U.S. nonfat dry milk
       fortified with vitamins A and D into the P.L. 480 program.

396.   U.S.D.A.   Economic Research Service. Agricultural-Food
       Policy Review. Washington, D.C.: USDA Economic Research
1977   Service. (NTIS PB-297 125/7 WF) 144 p.

       Provides American food policymakers with a convenient com-
       pilation of objective economic analyses of current policy
       issues. Serves as a 'briefing book' oriented toward the
       formulation of new national policies, programs and legis-
       lation, particularly the Agriculture and Consumer Protec-
       tion Act of 1977.

397.   U.S.D.A.   Economic Research Service. Analysis of Grain
       Reserves--A Proceedings,   ERS Report No. 634 by David J.
1976   Eaton and W. Scott Steele.   Washington D.C.: USDA, ERS.
       200 p.

       Provides a policy perspective on international and nation-
       al grain reserves. Contains five papers addressing the
       issue of international grain reserves and six papers on
       topics of national grain reserves.

398.   U.S.D.A. Economic Research Service. P.L. 480 Concessional
       Sales, Foreign Agricultural Economic Report No. 142. By
1977   Amalia Vellianitis-Fidas and Eileen Marsar Manfredi, For-
       eign Demand and Competition Division. Washington, D.C.:
       United States Department of Agriculture. 37 p.

       Reveiws: 1) the origin and history of Public Law (P.L.)
       480; 2) general and specific considerations in negotiating
       P.L. 480 agreements; and 3) procedures for implementing
       agreements. The glossary lists P L. 480 terminology.

399.   U.S.D.A.   Economic Research Service. The World Food Situ-
       ation and Prospects to 1985. Foreign Agricultural Economic
1974   Report No. 98. Washington, D.C.: USDA. 90 p.

       Comprehensive analysis of the "factors which influenced
       food production, consumption, and trade in the two decades
       prior to 1972, the causes for the turbulent developments
       of 1972-1974, and the main factors which will shape devel-
       opments in the next decade. Chapters 1, 2, and 3 review

past developments and the present situation. Chapter 4 contains projections of world food supply and demand to 1985. Chapter 5 discusses a key issue, grain stocks. Chapters 6 through 10 outline the issues surrounding nutritional levels and food aid; examine important factors influencing food supply and demand; and point out the differences among the less affluent countries of the world." Highlights policy issues raised by the nature and magnitude of bilateral and multilateral food aid programs. Updates the recommendations of the 1974 World Food Conference and provides a brief history of the Food Aid Convention. Concludes that "the goal of food self-sufficiency is not defensible" because "while there is clearly a need to produce much more food in many developing countries, the stimulation of food production without adequate attention to costs would reduce the general development of these countries and would conflict with the building of a more viable agricultural system, which is necessary if the world is to be fed adequately, efficiently and at the lowest cost."

401.
1980
United States Department of Agriculture, Economics, Statistics and Cooperatives Service. <u>Global Food Assessment, 1980</u>; Foreign Agricultural Economic Report No. 159. Washington, D.C.: U. S. Government Printing Office. 119 p.

Reports that world food production fell nearly 2.5 percent in 1979, the first decline in 7 years. Although output increased in South and Central America, it declined in most African countries and South Asia. Greatest food needs exist in the Sub-Saharan African regions and South Asia, but certain Central American, Caribbean, and South American countries will also require assistance. Presents data on food production and 1980 outlook for 79 low-and middle-income countries, reviews the 1979 food situation, and describes international and U.S. food aid policies.

402.
1980
U.S.D.A., Foreign Agricultural Service. "Food for Peace: The P.L. 480 Program." Washington, D.C.: USDA. July. 9 p.

Briefly describes the historical development of the P.L. 480 program and its benefits.

403.
1980
U.S.D.A., Foreign Agricultural Service. <u>Quarterly Report of the General Sales Manager, October 1 - December 31, 1979</u>. Washington, D.C.: Government Printing Office. 24 p.

Summarizes Title I, and III sales and Title II donations to foreign countries under P.L. 480 during the first quarter of U.S. fiscal 1980 (begins in October). Enumerates

P. L. 480 program problems caused by higher commodity prices. Highlights CCC Export Credit Sales programs. Provides useful tables such as P.L. 480 Title I, Concessional Sales Allocations Fiscal Year 1980 and P.L. 480 Exports First Quarter Fiscal 1980 by Country.

403.

1978

U.S.D.A., Office of the General Sales Manager. Public Law 480 Sales Program: A Brief Explanation of Title I." Washington, D.C.: U.S.D.A., Office of the General Sales Manager. 6 p.

Explains the mechanics and administration of Title I of the Public Law 480 Program. Discusses negotiation of P.L. 480 agreements, eligibility of commodity suppliers, financing and purchasing procedures and ocean transportation requirements.

404.

1979

U.S.D.A., Office of the General Sales Manager. <u>Public Law 480: Regulations Governing the Financing of Commercial Sales of Agricultural Commodities.</u> Washington, D.C.: GPO. 109 p.

Contains regulations governing the sale and exportation of agricultural commodities or products made available under Title I of the Agricultural Trade Development and Assistance Act of 1954 as amended in 1979. Under the Act, the Government of the United States enters into Agricultural Commodities Agreements with governments of the importing countries or private trade entities, covering financing of the sale and exportation of agricultural commodities and ocean transportation costs. Regulations cover: 1) the making of applications to the General Sales Manager for authorizations to purchase agricultural commodities; 2) the issuance of purchase authorizations by the General Sales Manager; and 3) the financing by Commodity Credit Corporation of the sale and exportation of these commodities through private trade channels to the maximum extent practicable.

405.

1975

U. S. GENERAL ACCOUNTING OFFICE. <u>Disincentives to Agricultural Production in Developing Countries: Report to the Congress.</u> Washington, D.C.: GPO. 117 p.

Discusses U.S. food aid policies and their impact on recipient nations from the vantage point of the donor. Concludes that U.S. agencies providing food and agricultural assistance should take steps to provide adequate incentives for growing more food.

406. U.S. GENERAL ACCOUNTING OFFICE, Comptroller General of the United States. <u>Increasing World Food Supplies--Crisis and Challenge</u>, Report to the Congress. Washington, D.C.: General Accounting Office. 72 p.

1974

Assessment of the world food situation and U.S. bilateral assistance to food and agriculture including P.L. 480, and USDA's Foreign Agricultural Service and Economic Research Service. Describes multilateral food assistance programs including the World Bank Group, Inter-American Development Bank, Asian Development Bank, African Development Bank and the WFP.

407. U. S. GENERAL ACCOUNTING OFFICE. <u>U. S. Participation in International Food Organizations: Problems and Issues.</u> Washington, D.C.: GPO. 27 p.

1976

Examines and evaluates major international food aid programs of the FAO, the WFP, and the World Food Council and their relationships to U.S. programs, institutions and agencies.

408. U.S. PANEL ON THE WORLD FOOD SUPPLY AND PRESIDENT'S SCIENCE ADVISORY COMMITTEE. <u>The World Food Problem: Volumes 1-3.</u> Washington, D.C.: GPO. 127 p., 772 p., and 332 p. respectively.

1967

Provides results of research conducted by more than one hundred individuals from federal agencies, universities, private foundations and industries who served on the President's (then Lyndon Johnson) Science Advisory Committee. Nutritional need, economic development and the task of technical assistance are discussed. Makes policy recommendations for increasing agricultural trade, cropland and co-op yields. Includes a brief discussion on the role of private enterprise and organizing for food policy changes. (Commonly known as the Bennett Report)

409. U. S. PRESIDENT. <u>The Food Aid Program 1966: Annual Report on Public Law 480.</u> Washington, D.C.: GPO. 158 p.

1967

Discusses major changes in P.L. 480 program such as: 1) the dropping of the surplus disposal concept in favor of the idea of producing enough food and fiber to meet necessary domestic, foreign, and reserve requirements; and 2) the new emphasis that P.L. 480 recipients make appropriate efforts to improve their own agricultural situation and bring food and population into balance. P.L. 480 sales totaled $1.52 billion in 1966. Thirty-seven Title I agreements were entered into with 16 countries during 1966. Other topics discussed include: the approval of 41 P.L. 480 loans to private business (private trade agreements) valued at $42.6 million to increase markets for U.S. agricultural products; balance-of-payments benefits; highlights of 1966 commodity programs; agricultural marketing and research; grants for economic development and emergency relief programs. Summarizes self-help projecs in India, Pakistan, Israel, Korea, Afghanistan, Iceland, Congo, Ghana, Morocco, Tunisia, Indonesia, Philippines and Vietnam. Contains over 90 pages of charts, tables and summaries of P.L. 480 amendments.

410. U. S. PRESIDENT. <u>Food for Freedom, New Emphasis on Self Help: 1967 Annual Report on Public Law 480.</u> Washington, D.C.: GPO. 160 p.

1968

In 1967, 39 Title I agreements were signed with developing countries valued at $1.2 billion. India accounted for nearly half. Approximately 2.4 million tons of food valued at $479 million were shipped under Title II. Barter contracts totaled $315.2 million. Describes the shift to dollar credit sales and discusses private trade agreements. Describes self-help programs in Afghanistan, Bolivia, Brazil, Ceylon, Chile, Colombia, Congo, Dominican Republic, Ghana, Guinea, Guyana, Iceland, India, Indonesia, Israel, Jordan, Korea, Liberia, Morocco, Pakistan, Paraguay, Sierra Leone, Somali Republic, Taiwan, Tunisia, Uruguay, and Vietnam. Contains over 80 pages of statistical data.

411. U. S. PRESIDENT. <u>Food for Peace: 1965 Annual Report on Public Law 480.</u> Washington, D.C.: GPO. 190 p.

1966

In 1965, Food for Peace shipments were 23 percent of total agricultural exports, the lowest since the beginning of the program in 1954. Exports under P.L. 480 in 1965 were $1.4 billion compared to $1.7 billion in 1964. During the year, 19 Title I agreements were signed for a market value of about $318 million. More than 1.2 million tons of food valued at $301.8 million were supplied under Title II. Barter contracts entered into in 1965 totaled $172 million, an increase of 26 percent over 1964. Other topics discussed include: the use and administration of foreign currencies, agricultural market development, common defense, grants for economic development, the WFP, and self-help activities. Contains 70 pages of statistical information on P.L. 480 aid to developing countries.

412. U. S. PRESIDENT. <u>Food for Peace: 1968 Annual Report on Public Law 480.</u> Washington, D.C.: GPO. 165 p.

1969

Food for Peace shipments in 1968 valued at $1.2 billion accounted for 19 percent of all U.S. agricultural exports. Report discusses new provision of the 1968 legislation with the primary aim of improving the U.S. balance of payments position. Highlights self-help programs in Afghanistan, Bolivia, Brazil, Chile, Colombia, Congo, Dominican Republic, Ghana, Guinea, Guyana, Iceland, India, Indonesia, Israel, Jordan, Korea, Liberia, Morocco, Pakistan, Paraguay, Sierra Leone, Somali Republic, Taiwan, Tunisia, Uruguay, and Vietnam. Discusses Title II agreements, market development programs, private trade agreements and barter program activity. Contains 70 pages of statistical data.

413.

1970

U. S. PRESIDENT. <u>1969 Annual Report on Public Law 480: Food for Peace.</u> Washington, D.C.: GPO. 147 p.

Nearly $905 million worth of P.L. 480 Title I aid and $256 million worth of Title II aid reached over 105 countries in 1969. Total P.L. 480 activity was $1,018 million accounting for 17 percent of total agricultural exports. Report discusses the programming process of Title II aid, private trade agreements, market development programs, grants for economic development and use of foreign currencies. Summarizes self-help programs in Bolivia, Dominican Republic, Ghana, India, Indonesia, Iran, Korea, Morocco, Paraguay and Vietnam. Contains over 50 pages of statistical data.

414.

1971

U. S. PRESIDENT. <u>1970 Annual Report on Public Law 480.</u> Washington, D.C.: GPO. 132 p.

P.L. 480 activity in 1970 leveled off at about $1 billion and provided U.S. balance of payments benefits of about a third of a billion dollars. Report discusses the continued hardening in terms under Title I sales programs, private trade agreements, market development activities, food for development, emergency relief programs and self-help programs in Brazil, Ghana, India, Indonesia, Korea and Vietnam. Contains 47 pages of statistical data.

415.

1972

U. S. PRESIDENT. [1971] <u>Annual Report on Agricultural Export Activities Carried Out Under Public Law 480 During Calendar Year 1971.</u> Washington, D.C.: GPO. 140 p.

Exports of agricultural commodities under P.L. 480 in calendar 1971 were valued at approximately $1 billion. Title I sales programs totaled $680 million and Title II donations rose to $291 million. Public Law 480 accounted for less than 13 percent of total U.S. agricultural exports in

1971. Report discusses private trade agreements, various sales programs and self-help projects in the Dominican Republic, Ghana, India, Indonesia, Morocco, Phillipines, Vietnam and Zaire. Summarizes WFP assistance and the status of the Food Aid Convention. Contains over 65 pages of statistical tables.

416. U. S. PRESIDENT. <u>1972 Annual Report on Public Law 480</u>. Washington, D.C.: GPO. 118 p.

1973

Exports of agricultural commodities under Public Law 480 in calendar 1972 were valued at slightly over $1 billion. Exports under Title I totaled $655 million and exports under Title II rose to $376 million. The year 1972 marked the first in which no local currency agreements could be entered into. P.L. 480 balance-of-payments benefits reached about $301 million. Report discusses various sales programs and self-help projects in Afghanistan, Bolivia, Dominican Republic, Ecuador, Ghana, Jordan, Korea, Morocco, Pakistan, Philippines, Tunisia, Vietnam and Zaire. Summarizes WFP assistance and the status of the Food Aid Convention. Contains nearly 50 pages of statistical data.

417. U. S. PRESIDENT. <u>1973 Annual Report on Public Law 480</u>. Washington, D.C.: GPO. 110 p.

1974

In calendar year 1973, exports of agricultural commodities under P.L. 480 were valued at approximately $750 million--a thirty percent decrease from the previous year. Title I shipments totaled $540 million and Title II shipments $210 million. Total balance-of-payments benefits in 1973 were $387 million. Discusses sales programs, private trade agreements and self help projects in Afghanistan, Cambodia, Indonesia, Pakistan, Sudan and South Vietnam. Summarizes WFP assistance and the status of the Food Aid Convention. Contains over 50 pages of statistical data.

418. U. S. PRESIDENT. [1974] <u>Food for Peace Program: 1974 Annual Report</u>. Washington, D.C.: GPO. 97 p.

1976

In a January 28, 1976 message to the Congress before the Committee on International Relations, President Gerald R. Ford transmitted the 1974 annual report on P.L. 480 (Food for Peace). He pointed out that in both East and West Africa, U.S. food aid represented about 40 percent of the total supplied by the international community. In calendar year 1974, exports of agricultural commodities under P.L. 480 were valued at approximately $760 million, a slight increase over calendar 1973's total of $750 million. Major

1974 food aid recipients were Vietnam. Cambodia, Bangladesh, Egypt, Chile and Pakistan. Provides summary and highlights of U.S. food aid program in underdeveloped countries and over 50 pages of statistical tables.

419. UNIVERSITY OF CALIFORNIA, Division of Agricultural Sciences. A Hungry World: The Challenge to Agriculture. Berkeley,
1974 CA: University of California, Berkeley, July. 327 p.

Assessment of global food production and distribution trends and implications for California and the world.

420. VALDES, Alberto; and HUDDLESTON, Barbara. Potential of Agricultural Exports to Finance Increased Food Imports in
1977 Selected Developing Countries. Washington, D.C.: International Food Policy Research Institute Occasional Paper No. 1. 72 p.

Suggests that the problem of financing adequate food imports may become a major barrier to adequate consumption in many developing countries. Examines the feasibility of financing additional food imports through agricultural exports. Provides trade and income data on 28 countries and conclusions about their future prospects.

421. VANKAI, Thomas A. "Czechoslovakia's 1976-80 Plan Sets High Aims for Farm Sector." Foreign Agriculture 15 (39): 8-10, September 26.

Examines the food and agricultural policies of Czechoslovakia's 1976-80 plan. The 5-year plan has set high farm sector targets, particularly for the output of food. Nevertheless, "even if planned increases are achieved, that country will have to import grain and oilseeds, with the United States as a major supplier."

422. WAGSTAFF, Howard. "Food Policies and Prospects--Insights from Global Modelling." Food Policy 4 (3): 155-168,
1979 August.

Examines the role of food trade under alternative future conditions of abundance and adversity based on a simulation model of the world economy developed by the Systems Analysis Research Unit (SARU) of the United Kingdom Department of the Environment. Other world food models are compared to SARU's model. Discusses the food policy issues of feed substitution, self-sufficiency, and food imports. The SARU model shows that a self-sufficiency strategy in the poorest regions leads to lower incomes and lower food consumption.

423.   WALLENSTEEN, Peter. "Scarce Goods are Political Weapons: The Case of Food." In The Political Economy of Food, pp.
1978   47-93. Edited by Vilo Harle. Farnborough, Hants, England: Saxon House, Teakfield Ltd.

Examines the historical use of food power by the United States beginning with a theoretical presentation of the conditions under which a given economic commodity can be turned into a political weapon. Investigates the circumstances leading to such a utilization of food and raises some propositions on possible counter measures.

424.   WALLERSTEIN, Mitchel B. "Foreign-Domestic Intersections in US Food Policy." Food Policy 5 (2): 83-96, May.
1980

Probes the major points of intersection between domestic and international food and agricultural policy in five areas: 1) the farm income/consumer price/food supply matrix; 2) international agricultural trade relations; 3) economic, strategic, and diplomatic uses of food resources; 4) LDC agricultural development and global food security; and 5) bilateral and multilateral food aid.

425.   WALLERSTEIN, Mitchel B.; and AUSTIN, James E. "The World Food Council at Three Years: Global Food System Manager?"
1978   Food Policy 3 (3): 191-201, August.

Discusses the Council's current role in international food policy making. Illuminates important food policy issues of the WFC--purportedly the highest international political body dealing exclusively with food and nutrition policy. Substantive issues discussed include production inputs, global food security, food aid, nutrition programming, and food trade. Describes the policy making process based on the results of the 1977 WFC's Third Ministerial Session in Manila. Includes a discussion of the role of WFC leadership, key country support, the Group of 77, the socialist nations, the United States, and the EEC and Japan.

426.   WHELAN, E. F. "Canada's Investment in World Agriculture." Agriculture Abroad 32 (6): 21-28, December.
1977

Brief discussion of Canada's food aid and development policies with particular reference to food and agricultural projects in developing countries.

427. WILLETT, Joseph W. *The World Food Situation: Problems and Prospects to 1985 Vol. I and II.* Dobbs Ferry, New York:
1976 Oceana, Publications, Inc. 1345 p.

Includes documents from the U.S. Department of Agriculture, the United Nations, the Food and Agriculture Organization, the University of California, Davis and the U.S. Agricultural Research Policy Advisory Committee (ARPAC). Most of the documents examine past trends in food production, trade, international food policies and the imbalance between developed and developing countries.

428. WINIKOFF, B. "Nutrition and Food Policy: the Approaches of Norway and the United States." *American Journal of Public Health*, 67: 552-7, June.
1977

Short, definitive analysis of the Norwegian Nutrition and Food Policy--a milestone in the practical formulation of governmentally sanctioned food policy. Compares specific nutritionally-oriented goals for Norwegians to the much more general and less efficient "Dietary Goals for the United States."

429. WITT, Lawrence W. "Development through Food Grants and Concessional Sales." In *Agriculture in Economic Development*, pp. 339-358. Edited by Carl Eicher and Lawrence Witt. New York: McGraw-Hill 415 p.
1964

Appraises P.L. 480 programs in Israel, Colombia, Pakistan, India and Tunisia. Examines the impact of food aid on the agricultural development of the recipients according to the policies of their governments, the relative strength and potential of the recipient's food sectors, and the effective administration of food aid programs.

430. WITT, Lawrence. "Discussion: Impact and Implications of Foreign Surplus Disposal on Underdeveloped Economies." *Journal of Farm Economics* 42 (5): 1046-1051, December.
1960

Discussion and review of two papers on the impact of P.L. 480 written by Dr. Theodore Schultz and Dr. S. R. Sen.

431. WITT, Lawrence. "Food Aid, Commercial Exports and the Balance of Payments." In *Food Policy: The Responsibility of the United States in the Life and Death Choices*, pp. 79-93. Edited by Peter G. Brown and Henry Shue. New York: The Free Press.

Examines the future of food aid in light of its limited availability after 1972. Argues that most of the changes in the volume of food aid can be explained by holding moral values on food aid constant in a framework of decreasing excess capacity and rising real costs of food aid. Describes four options of future food aid programming: 1) Embark upon an intermittent food aid program, one that takes effect only following years in which excess production permits low-cost concessional exports and donations; 2) Continue to operate at about the same level as in recent years, but at higher cost when necessary, saying that bargain foods are not the only reason for food aid; 3) Help food-deficit nations develop their internal capacity to produce food and to control population growth during an interim period gradually phasing out food aid activities; and 4) Make greater investments in developed countries which would enable them to expand population specifically for food aid exports. Concludes that "food-exporting countries are not likely to make these larger sacrifices unless there is greater comparability of sacrifice from people in other rich nations."

432. WITUCKI, Lawrence A. "Tanzania Boosts Food Output, Cuts Imports." Foreign Agriculture 16 (3): 10-11, January 16.

1978

Discusses Tanzania's agricultural and food policies, especially measures which led to a sharp reduction of U.S. agricultural imports from 1974 to 1977. Describes the impact of the Ujamaa (familyhood) program on agricultural production.

433. WORLD BANK. A Perspective on the Foodgrain Situation in the Poorest Countries, by S. J. Burki and T. J. Goering. World Bank Staff Working Paper No. 251. Washington, D.C.: World Bank, April. 43 p.

1977

Discusses development strategies for increased food production. Claims that "well-targeted external food aid programs which augment food consumption of the poor without diminishing incentives to domestic food production" could help solve malnutrition problems. Describes the Bank Group's leading programs for agriculture and foodgrain production.

434. WORLD FOOD CONFERENCE. Proceedings of the World Food Conference of 1976. Ames, Iowa: The Iowa State University Press. 685 p.

1976

A comprehensive collection of plenary and working papers, workshop reports and proceedings. Chapter three provides a general survey of the wide range of food policy issues affecting various nations. Chapter six summarizes national and international policy issues regarding food production, distribution and consumption.

435. WORLD FOOD PROGRAMME. Multilateral Food Aid--A Progress Report. *Agriculture Abroad* 32 (1) Supplement: 16 p.

1977

Description of the World Food Program and its achievements until 1976.

436. WORLD FOOD PROGRAMME. *Food Aid and Employment.* Rome, Italy: World Food Programme. 51 p.

1973

Discusses the impact of WFP food aid on the agricultural development of recipient countries and describes WFP programs and projects. Places emphasis on the relationship between food aid and rural employment in developing countries. Suggests that food aid contributes to the development of rural infrastructure and may have a positive production impact in the long run.

437. WORLD FOOD PROGRAMME. *Ten Years of World Food Programme Development Aid, 1963-72.* Rome, Italy: WFP. 72 p.

1973

Comprehensive review of objectives and activities of WFP covering 429 development projects involving $1.2 billion of WFP assistance in 94 countries and 159 emergency operations from 1963-72.

438. WORLD FOOD PROGRAMME, Committee on Food Aid Policies and Programmes. "Food Aid Policies and Programmes: A Survey of Studies of Food Aid." Rome, Italy: WFP/CFA (5/5-C). March. 69 p.

1978

Prepared by Professor Hans W. Singer of the Institute of Development Studies, University of Sussex, Brighton for the WFP Committee on Food Aid Policies and Programmes (CFA). Surveys "existing literature on food aid, with a view to synthesizing the empirical findings of case studies in recent years, and perhaps drawing generalized conclusions that would help in sharpening food aid priorities and operational guidelines for WFP and bilateral programmes."

439. WORLD FOOD PROGRAMME. Committee on Food Aid Policies and Programmes. "Terminal Report on Mali." Rome, Italy: FAO. 3 p.

1977

Brief description and assessment of WFP food aid programs in Mali, Africa promoting the production of domestic cereals.

440. WORLD FOOD PROGRAMME, Committee on Food Aid Policies and Porgrammes. "Studies of the Role of Food Aid in Relation to Trade and Agricultural Development in Botswana, Lesotho, and the Arab Republic of Egypt." Rome, Italy: WFP/CFA (1/10 Add. I). April 30 p.

1976

Study of constraints on agricultural development, including an assessment of the role of food aid. Study was carried out by the Government of Botswana during 1971/72 and is based on an extensive field survey of agricultural and livestock areas, both receiving and not receiving food aid. Study on Lesotho was carried out in 1975. Concludes that food aid did not constitute a major constraint to agricultural production in Botswana or Lesotho. Study on Egypt was carried out in 1974 and reviews the impact of a food project on agricultural production and income and concludes that a positive impact must either reduce imports or provide for higher exports.

441. WORLD FOOD PROGRAMME, Intergovernmental Committee. "The Contribution of Food Aid to the Improvement of Women's Status." Rome, Italy: WFP/IGC (27/15). February. 41 p.

1975

Examination of the part WFP has played in the advancement of women. Shows that food aid is potentially a useful form of aid by contributing to women's health, education, training and employment opportunities enabling women to contribute to development.

442. WORLD FOOD PROGRAMME, Intergovernmental Committee. "Food Aid and Habitat." Rome, Italy: WFP/IGC (1/15-B). February 31 p.

1976

Reviews impact of WFP food aid on agricultural settlements; house construction in rural areas; urban settlements; refugee settlements; and, disaster relief and rehabilitation following natural and man-made disasters. Concludes that food aid can be an additional capital resource for development in this sphere of activity, particularly through food for work projects.

443. WORTMAN, Sterling; and CUMMINGS, RALPH W. Jr. To Feed This World: The Challenge and the Strategy. Baltimore: The Johns Hopkins University Press. 440 p.

1978

Delineates the relationships between food and development pointing out the most promising approaches to rapid agricultural development. Demonstrates that economic and social justice, as well as prosperity, is in the long-run interest of society and calls for immediate strengthening of technical assistance efforts and financial aid through existing international banks and bilateral agencies. Encourages the continuation of humanitarian food aid programs and warns that "food aid programs which confuse humanitarin and political considerations and retard emergence of economically stronger trading partners are against the longer-term interest of both recipient and donor countries." Provides a good introduction to basic issues underlying food and agricultural policy.

444.   WOS, Augustryn; and GROCHOWSKI, Zdzislaw. "Agricultural Policies and General Economic Policy: The Polish Experi-
1977   ence." Food Policy 2 (1): 34-43, February.

Explains how socialist agricultural policies and planning takes place in relation to general economic policy combined with the influence of a controlled market. Discusses Polish agricultural economic growth and farmers and workers incomes.

445.   ZACHAR, G. "A Political History of Food for Peace." Cornell Agricultural Staff Paper, No. 77-18. Ithaca, New York:
1977   Cornell University, Department of Agricultural Economics, 36 p.

Historical review and analysis of the P.L. 480/Food for Peace Program. Discusses the political role of food aid in U.S. foreign policy and the establishment of U.S. international food policy.

AUTHOR'S GUIDE

Following is the most recent descriptive information supplied about the author at the time of publication.

ADCOCK, Robert E.: USDA Agricultural Attache, Kuala Lumpur.

AUSTIN, James E.: Associate Professor, Harvard Business School, Soldiers Field, Boston, Massachusetts 02163, USA, and Lecturer in Nutrition Policy and Programs, Harvard School of Public Health.

ARNOLD, Dr. Adlai F.: Employed by the ERS of the U.S. Department of Agriculture, he was stationed in Liberia with the U.S. gency for International Development as Policy and Planning Advisor to the Department of Agriculture. From 1965 to early 1970, he served as team leader of the U.S. Department of Agriculture PASA team with USAID in Paraguay. He received his Ph.D. degree in Agricultural Economics from Oklahoma State University in 1962, and is author of numerous reports on the agricultural problems of Paraguay.

ARROYO, Gonzalo: University of Paris, France.

AYERS, Alvin D.: Former Director, Far Eastern Regional Research Office, American Embassy, New Delhi, India.

BARD, Robert: A Professor of International Law at the University of Connecticut School of Law. Professor Bard's interest in food aid stemmed from his five years' service with the US Agency for International Development. He completed graduate work in economics and is studying the efficacy of commodity agreements to regulate agricultural trade for the benefit of developed and developing countries.

BELL, Richard E.: Former USDA Deputy Assistant Secretary of Agriculture for International Affairs and Commodity Programs.

BERGESEN, Helge Ole: Affiliated with the Norwegian Institute of International Affairs.

BHATTACHARJEE, J. P.: Dr. Bhattacharjee is Director of the Policy Analysis Division, FAO, Rome, Italy.

BIOLLEY, Vincent: Affiliated with the Office of U.S. Agricultural Attache, Rabat.

BLYTHE, Colin: Affiliated with the Social Nutrition Research Unit, Department of Nutrition, Queen Elizabeth College (University of London), Campden Hill, London. W8 FAH. In 1978,

he was a Visiting Research Fellow at the Institute of Nutrition Research, University of Oslo.

BRANNON, Russell H.: Faculty member of the Department of Agricultural Economics of the University of Kentucky and Associate Director of the University's Center for Developmental Change. As an agricultural specialist with the Ford Foundation, he acquired extensive experience in the agricultural problems of underdeveloped nations in Latin America. He received an M.A. in public administration from George Washington University and M.S. and Ph.D. degrees in agricultural economics from the University of Wisconsin.

BROWN, Lester R.: Senior Fellow of the Overseas Development Council and internationally recognized authority on agricultural development. Author of <u>Man, Land, and Foods</u>, <u>Seeds of Change</u>, <u>World Without Borders</u> and <u>In the Human Interest</u>.

BROWN, Peter G.: Director of the Center for Philosophy and Public Policy of the University of Maryland at College Park, USA. Author of numerous articles on the ethical problems of public policy.

BURKE, Melvin: Associate Professor of Economics, University of Maine.

BUZZANELL, Peter J.: Assistant U. S. Agricultural Attache in Brasilia.

CARBONELL, Jaffe: Affiliated with Fundacion Ciepe, Edf. Norte, Centro Simon Bolivar, Caracas, Venezuela.

CLAY, Edward J.: Affiliated with the Institute of Development Studies, University of Sussex, Brighton, United Kingdom.

COHN, Theodore: Associate Professor of Political Science at Simon Fraser University in Burnaby, British Columbia. He teaches international politics and Canadian foreign policy. He received his Ph.D. from the University of Michigan. He has written a number of articles on international aid and trade, and has done extensive interviewing at the World Bank, Canadian government agencies, and nongovernmental organizations. He is currently involved in a research project on political aspects of Canadian trade.

COLLINS, Joseph: Co-founder of the Institute for Food and Development Policy, located in San Francisco and New York, USA. Dr. Collins has studied and traveled extensively in the Third World during the past twenty years. He completed graduate studies in public policy at Columbia University and the Institute for Policy Studies. He collaborated with Richard Barnet and Ronald Mueller in researching Global Reach: The Power of the Multinational Corporation.

COOLIDGE, Frank A.: Assistant US Agricultural Attache, London, UK.

CROUCH, Luis: Professor, Instituto Superior de Agricultura, Santiago de los Caballeros, Dominican Republic.

De JANVRY, Alain: Professor, Department of Agriculture and Resource Economics, 207 Giannini Hall, University of California, Berkeley, Berkeley, California 94720, USA.

DeMARCO, Susan: Affiliated with the Agribusiness Accountability Project, 1000 Wisconsin Avenue, N.W. Washington, D.C., 20007, USA.

DEQUIN, Horst: A consultant to the Technical Assistance Program of the Federal Republic of Germany, he conducted a general agro-economic survey of Malawi from 1965-1967.

DIRKS, Harlan J.: A member of the US State Department's Senior Seminar in foreign policy and US Agricultural Attache, Canberra, Australia.

DUNCAN, E. R.: Coordinating Editor, University of Mid-America.

ECKHOLM, Erik P.: Associate Fellow with the Overseas Development Council.

EHMAN, Frank W.: US Agricultural Attache, Bern.

El-SHERBINI, Aziz: Chief, FAO/ECWA Agricultural Division, c/o UNDP, Post Box 4656, Beirut, Lebanon.

ESKILDSEN, C. R.: Associate Administrator, FAS, USA.

FAMORIYO, Segun: Dr. Famoriyo is with the Nigerian Institute of Social and Economic Research, University of Ibadan, Ibadan, Nigeria.

FENDER, Frank: Assistant to the Director of International Programs in Agriculture at Purdue University, USA.

FIENUP, Darrell F.: Program Advisor in Agriculture for the Ford Foundation and Professor of Agricultural Economics at the University of Minnesota, USA. He received a master's degree in agicultural economics from Montana State University and a doctorate in economics from the University of Wisconsin. At the Ford Foundation, Dr. Fienup was charged with the develpment of the company's agricultural programs in Chile, Argentina, Uruguay, and Paraguay.

FITZGERALD, D. A.: Served in various capacities in the U.S.D.A. from 1936 to 1946 and in the International Cooperation Administration and its predecessors from 1948 to 1962. He served as Secretary-General of the International Emergency Food Council from 1946 to 1948. Mr. FitzGerald joined the staff of The Brookings Institution in 1962 to undertake an examination of the policy and operational issues involved in U.S. foreign economic aid, especially to developing countries.

FLOTO, Edgardo: The author is with the Centre of Latin-American Studies, University of Cambridge, History Faculty Building, West Road, Cambridge CB39EF, United Kingdom.

FOWELLS, H. A.: Foreign Research and Technical Division, Agricultural Research Service, USA.

FREEMAN, Orville L.: Former, US Secretary of Agriculture.

FRIEDMANN, Karen J.: Now retired, she is an agricultural economist formerly with the Food Research Institute, Stanford University and the FAS, USDA.

GEORGE, Susan: A graduate of Smith College, where she was elected to Phi Beta Kappa, she received a "Licence" in philosophy from the Sorbonne. She recently completed a doctorate at the Ecole des Hautes Etudes en Sciences Sociales of the University of Paris. She was an active militant in the anti-Vietnam-war struggle and has been a Fellow of the Transnational Institute since 1973. She participated in preparing the TNI counter-report for the World Food Conference _World Hunger: Causes and Remedies_. Her subsequent work on food issues led to publication of her 1976 book, _How the Other Half Dies: The Real Reasons for World Hunger_, which has been reprinted several times in the US and Great Britain and translated into numerous foreign languages.

GHOSH, Rabindra Nath: Department of Economics, University of Western Australia.

GILBERT, Alvin E.: US Agricultural Attache at Islamabad.

GIRDNER, JANET: Department of Political Science, Iowa State University of Science and Technology, Ames, Iowa, 50011, USA.

GOERING, Theodore J.: Professor, University of California, Berkeley, USA.

GOLDICH, Judith G.: An international economist with the Centrally Planned Economies Division, FAS, USDA.

GRAY, Roger: Professor at the Food Research Institute, Stanford University, Stanford, California, 94305, USA.

GREENSHIELDS, Bruce L.: A member of the Foreign Demand and Competition Division, ERS, USDA.

GRIFFIN, Philip: The author is attached to the Ministry of Agriculture in Dublin, Ireland, where he is First Vice Chairman of the governing committee of the World Food Programme (Committee on Food Aid Policies and Programmes). He visited Peru in 1976 as leader of a UN team evaluating WFP projects, and returned there in 1977 for the OECD Development Centre to study the impact of food aid on the country.

GROCHOWSKI, Zdzislaw: Affiliated with the Institute of Agricultural Economics, Warszawa, Poland.

GUSTAFSSON, Mervi: Affiliated with the Tampere Peace Research Institute, Finland.

GWATKIN, Davidson R.: A Senior Fellow at the Overseas Development Council, 1717 Massachusetts Avenue NW, Washington, DC, 20036, USA.

HALLOWELL, Elmer W.: U. S. Agricultural Attache in Rome, Italy.

HARLE, Vilo: A member of the Food Study groups, International Peace Research Association, University of Tampere, Tampere, Finland.

HATHAWAY, Dale E.: Former Assistant Secretary of Agriculture for International Affairs and Commodity Programs.

HEADY, Earl O.: Curtiss Distinguished Professor of Economics and Executive Director of the Center for Agricultural and Rural Development at Iowa State University, Ames, Iowa, USA.

HOWARD, James O.: U. S. Agricultural Attache in Pretoria, South Africa.

HUGHES, T. Walter: A staff member of the Program Development Division, FAS, USDA.

HUTCHINS, James A. Jr.: USDA, Assistant Sales Manager, Export Marketing Service.

ISENMAN, Paul J.: Affiliated with the US Agency for International Development and a Visiting Fellow at the Institute of Development Studies, University of Sussex, UK.

ISHIKAWA, Shigeru: Consultant, the Asian Development Bank and Professor at Hitotsubashi University, Japan.

IVERSON, K. L.: Affiliated with the Department of Statistics and Community Health, Trinity College at the time this study was written. He may now be reached at 4914 Foxden Court, Charlotte, North Carolina, 28212, USA.

IVERSON, S. C.: Currently with the Department of Urban and Environmental Engineering, University of North Carolina, UNCC Station, Charlotte, North Carolina, 28223, USA.

JOHNSON, D. Gale: Professor of Economics at the University of Chicago, Illinois, USA.

JONSSON, U.: Affiliated with the Tanzania Food and Nutrition Centre, Box 977, Dar es Salaam, Tanzania.

KAHN, Kabir-ur-Rahman: Lecturer, Department of Public International Law, University of Edinburgh, Old College South Bridge, Edinburgh, EH 8 9YL, U.K.

KANEDA, Hiromitsu: Professor of Economics, University of California, Davis, USA.

KEVANY, J. P.: Affiliated with the Department of Community Health, Trinity College, Dublin 2, Eire.

KOFI, Tetteh A.: Formerly an Assistant Professor of the Food Research Institute of Stanford University, Dr. Kofi is presently a Professor of Economics at the University of Notre Dame, Indiana, 46556, USA. His major research interest is the economic development of Third World countries with emphasis on the economics of commodity markets. He is conducting a study of the world cocoa industry, concentrating on price determination and the performance of commodity exchanges and terminal markets. To this end he conducted a two-month study in Brazil, Ecuador, and Colombia to gather materials on cocoa, which will result in a forthcoming book, The Political Economy of the World Cocoa Industry. Dr. Kofi has served as consultant to the United Nations Conference on Trade and Development, the World Bank, and the Government of Ghana.

KRIESBERG, Martin: Coordinator, International Organization Affairs in USDA's International Development Division.

KUO-CHUN, Chao: Head of East Asia Department, Indian School of International Studies, University of Delhi, India.

LAPPE, Frances Moore: Co-founder of the Institute for Food and Development Policy, located in San Francisco and New York, USA. She has published numerous articles in academic and popular journals, lectured all over the world, and is also the author of <u>Diet for a Small Planet</u>.

LIBBIN, Susan A.: An international economist with the Statistics Program Area, Foreign Demand and Competition Division, ERS, USDA.

LIPTON, Michael: Professor at the Institute of Development Studies, University of Sussex, Falmer, Brighton Sussex, England, BN1 9RF.

MANN, Jitendar S.: Research Associate in agricultural economics at the University of Minnesota, USA.

MAXWELL, Simon: An agricultural economist with the British Tropical Agricultural Mission, Casilla 359, Santa Cruz, Bolivia. At the time the article was written in 1978, he was a temporary research officer at the Institute of Development Studies, University of Sussex, Brighton, UK.

MAYER, Jean: President, Tufts University, Medford, Massachusetts, 02155, USA.

McNITT, Harold A.: Staff member of the Foreign Demand and Competition Division, ERS, USDA.

MEAD, Arthur: Assistant Administrator of P. L. 480 Programs, FAS, USDA.

MIELKE, Myles: An economist with the Foreign Demand and Competition Division, ERS, USDA.

MINEAR, Larry: As a Consultant on World Hunger to Church World Service and Lutheran World Relief, Mr. Minear represents these agencies in discussions on food policy at the United Nations and in Washington, D.C. He was actively involved in the World Food Conference at Rome. Trained at Yale and Harvard in theology and history, he has a background in social studies teaching, domestic anti-poverty programs and work in Africa.

MISSIAEN, Edmond: Staff member of the Foreign Demand and Competition Division, ERS, USDA.

MORRIS, Roger: A former member of the US State Department, on the National Security Council Staff, and a legislative assistant in the U.S. Senate.

MURRAY, Kenneth L.: US Agricultural Attache, Abidjan, Ivory Coast.

NEUNTEUFEL, Marta: Affiliated with the Food and Agriculture Program, at the International Institute for Applied Systems Analysis, 2361 Laxenburg, Austria.

NG, Gek-boo: At the time the article was written, the author was with the World Employment Programme of the International Labour Office in Geneva. He is currently Deputy Director, ILO Area Office, P. O. Box 2061, Dacca, Bangladesh.

OLORUNSOLA, Victor: Chairperson and Professor, Departmtne of Political Science, Iowa State University of Science and Technology, Ames, Iowa, 50011, USA.

PAYNE, P. R.: Reader in Applied Nutrition, London School of Hygiene and Tropical Medicine, London, UK.

PECK, Anne: Associate Professor at the Food Research Institute, Stanford University, Stanford, California, 94305, USA.

PHILLIPS, Don: Staff member, Grain and Feed Division, FAS, USDA.

RAO: V.K.R.V.: This article was prepared during author's brief assignment as Senior Policy Adviser with the United Nations Institute for Social Development.

RECHCIGL, Miloslav Jr.: A Nutrition advisor and Acting Director of the Office of Research in the Agency for International Development, US Department of State. He has a B.S. in Biochemistry, a Master of Nutritional Science degree, and a Ph.D. in nutrition, biochemistry and physiology, all from Cornell University. He was formerly a Research Biochemist in the National Cancer Institute, National Institutes of Health and subsequently served as Special Assistant for Nutrition and Health in the Health Services and Mental Health Administration, US Department of Health, Education, and Welfare.

ROGERS, Keith D.: Research Associate, Center for Agricultural and Rural Development, Iowa State University, Ames, Iowa, USA.

ROTHMAN, Harry: Affiliated with the Department of Liberal Studies in Science, University of Manchester, England.

SANDERSON, Fred: Affiliated with the Brookings Institution, 1775

Massachusetts Avenue NW, Washington, D.C., 20036, USA. He directed a project for the Brookings Institution on "World Agriculture: Reassessment of Trends and Policies." He is a former director of the US State Department's Office of Food Policy, and a member of its planning staff.

SCHMITT, Bernard A.: An economist with the US Congress Joint Committee on Taxation. He received his Ph.D. from Florida State University and served as a research economist with the Florida State Department of Commerce.

SCHNEIDER, WILLIAM, Jr.: Affiliated with the Hudson Institute, Croton-on-Hudson, New York 10520, USA.

SCHUH, Dr. G. Edward: Deputy Assistant Secretary for International Affairs and Commodity Programs, USDA.

SCHULTZ, Theodore: Affiliated with the University of Chicago.

SCHWARZ, Reinhold: A professional agriculturalist in the Office of the US Agricultural Attache, Bern, Switzerland.

SECHLER, Susan: Affiliated with the Agribusiness Accountability Project, 1000 Wisconsin Avenue, NW, Washington, D.C., 20007 USA.

SEN, S. R.: A member of the Indian Planning Commission, New Delhi, India.

SHAW, D. J.: Senior Lecturer in Rural Economy University of Khartoum.

SHEETS, Hal: A 1973 graduate from Reed College, USA.

SHUE, Henry: Research Associate of the Center for Philosophy and Public Policy of the University of Maryland at College Park, USA. Author of a number of articles on the ethical problems of public policy.

SINGER, H. W.: A Professorial Fellow, Institute of Development Studies, University of Sussex, UK.

SINHA, Radha: A faculty member of Glasgow University, Department of Political Economy, Adam Smith Building, University of Glasgow, G128RT, United Kingdom. He was Visiting Professor at Nanzan University and the Institute of Economic Research Hitotsubashi University, Japan. He has also served as a consultant to the Food and Agricultural Organization of the United Nations.

SORENSON, Vernon L.: A Professor in Agricultural Economics, Michigan State University, USA. His teaching program includes

Agricultural Trade Policy and Policy Issues in Food Systems. He obtained his Ph.D. from the University of Minnesota and received the American Agricultural Economics Association national award for an outstanding Ph.D. dissertation. He has since made numerous contributions to agricultural trade policy formulation through his research and participation in government. He served as a foreign service officer of the US Department of State in 1964-65, during which time he dealt primarily with agricultural policy conflicts.

STAM, Jerome M.: At the time of this writing, Mr. Stam was a graduate student in Agricultural Economics at Michigan State University, USA.

STEVENS, Christopher: Research Officer at the Overseas Development Institute, 10-11 Percy Street, London, W1P, OJB, United Kingdom.

STOKEY, Edith: Professor at the Kennedy School of Government, Harvard University, Cambridge, Massachusetts, USA.

TALBOT, Ross B.: Professor of Political Science at Iowa State University of Science and Technology, 503 Ross Hall, Ames, Iowa, 50011, U.S.A.

TIMMER, C. Peter: H. E. Babcock Professor of Food Economics, Division of Nutritional Science, Cornell University, Ithaca, New York, 14850, USA.

TOLLEY, George S.: Professor of Economics at the University of Chicago, Chicago, Illinois, USA. At the time of writing, he was on leave as Deputy Assistant Secretary, for Tax Policy of the US Treasury. Prior to joining the Chicago faculty in 1966, he held an executive position in the USDA with responsibilities for economic development of non-metropolitan parts of the economy. He obtained M.A. and Ph.D. degrees from the University of Chicago. His field of research and writing include agricultural economics, economic development, urban economics, natural resources and environmental problems, monetary fiscal policy and consumer demand. He has served as consultant to the Ministry of Agriculture of the Republic of Korea, Minister of Planning of Panama, International Bank for Reconstruction and Development, University of Puerto Rico, Applachia Commission, and the President's Commission on Rural Poverty.

TOMA, Peter A.: Peter Toma joined the faculty of the University of Arizona Department of Government in 1959. He was a member of the USAID research mapping team on Food for Peace in 1964-65. He held the Haynes Fellowship while working toward a Ph.D. at the University of Southern California and is a specialist in communist systems and developing areas. Professor Toma is also the editor of the text, <u>Basic Issues in International Relations.</u>

TRURAN, James A.: A former Assistant US Agricultural Attache, Brasilia, Brazil.

TUOMI, Helena: Affiliated with the University of Tampere, Finland.

VANKAI, Thomas: Agricultural economist with the Foreign Demand and Competition Division, ERS, USDA.

WAGSTAFF, Howard: A lecturer in agricultural economics at the University of Edinburgh, Kings Buildings, West Mains Road, Edinburgh EH9 3JG, UK.

WALLENSTEEN, Peter: Affiliated with Uppsala University, Sweden.

WALLERSTEIN, Mitchel B. (Dr.): Assistant Professor of the International Nutrition Program and Department of Political Science, Massachusetts Institute of Technology, Cambridge, Massachusetts, 02139, USA.

WILLETT, Joseph W.: Director, Foreign Demand and Competition Division, ERS, USDA.

WITUCKI, Lawrence A.: An agricultural economist with the Foreign Demand and Competition Division, ERS, USDA.

WOS, Augustyn: Affiliated with the Institute of Agricultural Economics, Warszawa, Poland.

DIRECTORY OF FOOD AID AND DEVELOPMENT AGENCIES

Many United States and other international agencies involved in the distribution or coordination of food or development aid to Third World nations are listed here. Emphasis is placed on governmental and private organizations which have a significant impact on the formulation of food policy and the distribution of domestic and international food aid. The list is by no means exhaustive. It is a handy list of the major agencies and organizations for researchers, scholars, government officials and concerned individuals who want to know more about the specific operation of international food aid and development programs.

INTERNATIONAL NON-GOVERNMENTAL ORGANIZATIONS

AFRICA COMMITTEE FOR THE REHABILITATION OF SOUTHERN SUDAN (ACROSS)
    c/o Medical Assistance Programs
    P.O. Box 50
    Wheaton, Illinois 60187 USA

    Established in 1972, this coalition of nine Protestant missionary groups in the US, West Germany, Australia, and Sweden, operates agricultural projects in the southern Sudan.

BROTHERS TO ALL MEN (BAM)
    9, rue de Savoie
    75006 Paris, France
    033-05-71

    Established in 1965, BAM sponsors a volunteer service

program for young men to work on agricultural development projects in Brazil, Ecuador, India, Peru, Upper Volta, and other developing countries.

CARIBBEAN FOOD CROPS SOCIETY
P. O. Box H
Rio Piedras, Puerto Rico 00928
(809) 766-2331

Established in 1963, the agency's purpose is to "advance Caribbean food production and distribution in all their aspects to the end of improving levels of nutrition and standards of living." Over 25 countries in the Caribbean are members.

CARITAS INTERNATIONALIS: INTERNATIONAL CONFEDERATION OF CATHOLIC CHARITIES
16, Piazza S. Calisto
00153 Rome, Italy
(06) 6984597

Established in 1951, this international confederation of Roman Catholic organizations provides emergency relief and food aid to poverty areas throughout the world. Publication: _Intercaritas_ (quarterly).

THE CLUB OF ROME
Via Giorgione 163
147 Rome, Italy
U.S. Association: 1735 DeSales St. N.W.
Washington, D.C. 20036
(202) 638-1029

International forum on global issues, including the relationships among food, population, and other resources. Established in 1968. Publications: _World Dynamics_, _The Limits to Growth_ (1972); _Mankind at the Turning Point: The Second Report to the Club of Rome_.

FRIENDS WORLD COMMITTEE FOR CONSULTATION (FWCC)
Right Sharing of World Resources (RSWR)
1506 Race Street
Philadelphia, Pennsylvania 19102

Established in 1937, FWCC is the international organization of the Religious Society of Friends (Quakers). It maintains a small fund for the support of agricultural development projects in underdeveloped nations.

INTERNATIONAL ASSOCIATION OF AGRICULTURAL ECONOMISTS (IAALD)
Dartington House
Little Clarendon Street
Oxford OCI, 2HP, England

Established in 1929, the IAALD attempts to "foster the application of the science of agricultural economics in the improvement of the economic and social conditions of rural people and their associated communities; to advance knowledge of agricultural processes and the economic organization of agriculture; and to facilitate communication and exchange of information."

INTERNATIONAL CENTER OF TROPICAL AGRICULTURE (CIAT)
Apartado Aereo 6713
Cali, Colombia

Established in 1968 to improve agricultural production in the lowland tropics of the Western Hemisphere.

INTERNATIONAL FEDERATION OF AGRICULTURAL PRODUCERS (IFAP)
1, rue de Hauteville
75010 Paris, France

Established in 1946, IFAP is composed of farmers' associations in 44 countries. It provides a forum and acts as a spokesperson for its member organizations. Concerns have included agricultural production in developing countries, agrarian reform, cooperatives, food aid policy, agricultural development assistance and international agricultural trade. Publications: IFAP News (monthly); World Agriculture (quarterly); and various conference reports.

LUTHERAN WORLD FEDERATION (LWF)
Department of World Service
150, route de Ferney
1211 Geneva 20, Switzerland
022-33-34-00

Established in 1947, the LWF provides emergency food aid and operates agricultural rehabilitation and development projects to more than 45 countries in Africa, Asia, and Latin America through its component part, Lutheran World Service.

OXFAM
> 274 Banbury Road
> Oxford OX 2 7D2, England
> 0865 56777
>
> U. S. Oxfam-America Office:
> 302 Columbus Avenue
> Boston, Massachusetts 02116
> (617) 247-3304
>
> Established in 1942, OXFAM is an international relief and development agency providing funding to groups working in more than 80 countries. It supports food relief, food production, food storage, and agricultural projects. Regional offices are maintained in India, Indonesia, Malawi, Ethiopia, Upper Volta, Togo, Brazil, Peru, Barbados and Zaire. Publication: <u>OXFAM News</u> (bimonthly).

WORLD COUNCIL OF CHURCHES (WCC)
> 150, route de Ferney
> 1211 Geneva 20, Switzerland
> 33-34-00
>
> Established in 1948, WCC is an organization of churches in over 90 countries representing the major Protestant and Orthodox denominations. The WCC provides emergency food relief to developing countries through its Commission on Inter-Church Aid, Refugee and World Service (CICARWS) and provides grants and loans to select agricultural projects.

WORLD ASSOCIATION FOR THE STRUGGLE AGAINST HUNGER (ASCOFAM)
> 163-165, avenue Charles de Gaulle
> 9220 Neuilly-sur-Seine, France
>
> Established in 1957, ASCOFAM is concerned with promoting agricultural and food policies and programs to combat hunger in the world.

PRIVATE OR GOVERNMENTAL ORGANIZATIONS BY COUNTRY

ARGENTINA
> Asociacion Argentina de Nutricion (Argentine Nutricion Association)
> Santa Fe 1171
> Buenos Aires, Argentina
> 89-06-21

AUSTRALIA

Australian Development Assistance Agency
Canberra, A.C.T., Australia

Government international aid organization.

Community Aid Abroad (CAA)
75 Brunswick Street
Fitzroy, Victoria 3065, Australia

Established in 1953, CAA provides emergency food aid and agricultural development assistance to projects in developing countries.

BANGLADESH

Bangladesh Agricultural Research Council
130/C Road #1, Dhanmandi Residential Area
Dacca-5, Bangladesh

BELGIUM

Ministry of Development Cooperation
Brussels, Belgium

The government's international development agency.

International Cooperation for Social and Economic Development (CIDSE)
59-61, avenue Adolph Lacomble
1040 Brussels, Belgium
02-36-57-98

BRAZIL

Comissao Nacional de Alimentacao (National Food Commission) (CNA)
Av. Rio Branco
Rio de Janeiro, G.B., Brazil

CANADA

Canadian Hunger Foundation
75 Sparks Street
Ottawa, Ontario K1P 5A6
(613) 237-0180

Conducts educational programs on the world food problem and provides agricultural development assistance to developing countries.

Canadian International Development Agency (CIDA)
122 Bank Street
Ottawa, Ontario K1A 0G4
(613) 966-7761

CIDA is a federal government program which funds and coordinates major bilateral food aid or food-related development projects in Bangladesh, India, Malaysia, Sri Landa, Algeria, Morocco, Tunisia, Upper Volta, Mali, Mauritania, Niger, Chad, Senegal, Rwanda, Zaire, Madagascar, Ghana, Tanzania, Kenya, Guyana, the Leeward and Windward Islands, El Salvador, Honduras and Peru. Its "Strategy for International Development Cooperation, 1975-1980" charges the country with the goal of providing "a substantial program of food aid, including the provision of one million tons of grain per year." Canada's food aid policy favors agricultural development rather than emergency food relief. CIDA provides multilateral food aid through the WFP of the United Nations. It provides technical or capital assistance to agricultural development projects through the World Bank, the UN Development Program, UNICEF, the Asian Development Bank, African Development Bank, Caribbean Development Bank and Inter-American Development Bank. CIDA works in conjunction with the Consultative Group on International Agricultural Research. Pub. <u>Canada: Strategy for International Development Cooperation</u>, 1975-1980 (1975); <u>Annual Review: Cooperation Canada</u> (bimonthly); <u>Contact</u> (monthly).

Christian Reformed World Relief Committee of Canada Committee of Canada
P. O. Box 235
Grimsby, Ontario L3M 4G3
(416) 643-2507

See index for Christian Reformed World Relief Committee, USA.

Cooperative for American Relief Everywhere (CARE)
CARE of Canada
1312 Bank Street
Ottawa, Ontario K1S 5H7

See index for Cooperative for American Relief Everywhere, USA.

Department of Agriculture (Agriculture Canada)
Sir John Carling Building
Ottawa, Ontario K1A 0C5
(613) 994-5533

A federal agency which is responsible for food policy development and coordination of regulatory activities focused on Canadian agriculture and the provision of food assistance to developing countries.

Food for the Hungry
P. O. Box 67800
Vancouver, British Columbia V5X 3L8
(604) 324-7885

Also known as Dominion Food for the Hungry Society, this organization provides food aid and agricultural development assistance to Kenya, Ethiopia, Niger, Mauritania, Senegal, Bangladesh, India, Costa Rica, Haiti, Honduras, Panama, Nicaragua, Vietnam, Guatemala and other developing countries.

COLOMBIA
    Instituto Nacional de Nutricion (National Institute of Nutrition)
    Carretera 3, no. 18-24, A. A.
    15609 Bogota, E. E., Colombia

CZECHOSLOVAKIA
    Czechoslovakia National Committee of Nutrition
    Czechoslovakia Academy of Sciences
    Budejovicka 800
    Prague, Czechoslovakia

DENMARK
    Afdelingen for Internationalt Udviklings-samarbejde
    (Danish International Development Agency) (DANIDA)
    Amaliegade 7
    1256 Copenhagen K. Denmark

    The Danish government's international development agency. It provides bilateral food aid to developing countries.

ECUADOR
    Instituto Nacional de Nutricion (INN)
    Avenida Colombia
    Quito, Ecuador

FRANCE
> Ministry of Cooperation
> Paris, France
>
> The French government's international development agency.

GERMANY, FEDERAL REPUBLIC OF
> Ministry of Economic Cooperation
> Kaiserstrasse 185-197
> 53 Bonn, West Germany
>
> The German government's international development agency which monitors and funds food aid and food-related development projects in developing countries.

ISRAEL
> Ministry of Foreign Affairs
> International Cooperation Division
> Jerusalem, Israel
>
> Administers the foreign aid program.

JAPAN
> Japan International Cooperation Agency
> No. 42, Honmura-Cho, Ichigaya, Shinjuku-ku
> Tokyo, Japan
>
> The Japanese government's international development agency.

MEXICO
> Coordination of Initiatives for Human Development in Latin
>   America (CIDAL)
> Apartado 42, Suc. "A"
> Cuernavaca, Morelos, Mexico
> 2-40-41

NETHERLANDS
> Ministry of Development Assistance
> The Hague, Netherlands
>
> The government's international development agency.

NORWAY

        Direktoratet for Utviklingshjelp (Norwegian Agency for International Development) (NORAD)
        Postboks 8142
        Oslo-Dep., Oslo 1, Norway

        The Norwegian government's international development agency.

SWEDEN

        Styrelsen for Internationell Utveckling
          (Swedish International Development Authority) (SIDA)
        Birger Jarlsgatan 61,
        105 25 Stockholm, Sweden

        The Swedish government's international development agency.

UNION OF SOVIET SOCIALIST REPUBLICS (USSR)
        Institute of Nutrition
        Ustinsky pr. 2/14
        Moscow G-240, USSR

UNITED KINGDOM
        Ministry of Overseas Development
        Eland House, Stag Place
        London, S. W. 1, England

        The British government's international development agency.

UNITED STATES

Government Organizations

AGENCY FOR INTERNATIONAL DEVELOPMENT (AID)
        320 21st St. N.W.
        Washington, D.C. 20523 USA
        (202) 632-8628

AID's Office of Food for Peace administers Title II of P.L. 480 and works in conjunction with the USDA to administer Title I P.L. 480 food aid sales. In fiscal year, 1978, all Food for Peace Programs (P.L. 480) provided $1.06 billion worth of food aid to developing countries. AID's development assistance programs attempt to increase food production, improve nutrition, and enhance the quality of life for the rural poor in developing countries. They are coordinated by the AID Bureau for Technical Assistance, its Office of Agriculture and Office of Nutrition. Food and nutrition activities amounted to 40% of AID's budget for fiscal year 1978. AID makes food aid allocations to the World Food Programme and other intergovernmental organizations concerned with the international food problems such as the International Fund for Agricultural Development, the UN Development Programme, UNICEF, FAO and OAS. Publications: <u>Front Line</u> (bi-weekly newsletter; <u>AID Research and Development Abstracts</u> (quarterly; <u>War on Hunger</u> (monthly); <u>Catalog of Selected Aid Publications</u> (1974); and various other publications and reports listed in the bibliography.

CONGRESSIONAL BUDGET OFFICE (CBO)
    House Annex #2
    2nd and D Street, S.W.
    Washington, D.C. 20515
    (202) 225-4546

Performs formal analyses of major budget issues, including issues of domestic and international food aid, before the United States Congress.

DEPARTMENT OF AGRICULTURE (USDA)
    14th Street & Independence Ave., S.W.
    Washington, D.C. 20250
    (202) 447-4026

Consists of several agencies concerned with international food aid and food policy: The Agricultural Research Service (ARS) is the chief research agency of the USDA and its International Programs Division administers foreign research grants and contracts under Public Law 480, and coordinates other USDA activities in international economic, technical, and cooperative assistance. The Commodity Credit Corporation of the USDA determines the availability of US agricultural commodities for sale to foreign governments, authorizes P.L. 480 sales and provides funding for P.L. 480 shipments. The Foreign Agricultural Service of the USDA administers the system of agricultural attaches in US embassies, and assists in the development of US international trade policy for agricultural commodities, including the P.L. 480 sales. The Economic Research Service (ERS) carries out research on worldwide and domestic supply and demand conditions, and the impact of US and foreign policies on world farm trade. The ERS also conducts international training programs in agricultural administration, policy, economics and agricultural development and coordinates

USDA's relations with FAO, the World Bank, OECD, and other intergovernmental agencies. Publications: <u>Foreign Agriculture Circular</u> series; <u>Agricultural Economics Research</u> (quarterly); and a variety of other pertinent publications listed in this bibliography.

DEPARTMENT OF STATE
    Office of Food Policy and Programs (OFP)
    2201 C Street, N.W.
    Washington, D.C. 20520

The OFP is divided into two divisions responsible for formulating US foreign policy on world food issues and coordinating the State Department's sale of agricultural commodities and provision of international food aid. The Food for Freedom Division (OFP/FFD) formulates the Department's position on food aid agreements; develops the eligibility requirements for disbursement of US food aid to developing countries; and establishes self-help, marketing requirements, export limitation, and purchase requirements of US food aid agreements. The Division also formulates US food aid policy and conducts consultations on US food aid programs with other food exporting countries. The OFP/FFD coordinates the Department's participation in the Inter-Agency Staff Committee on Food Aid and the FAO Subcommittee on Surplus Disposal.

The Food Policy Division (OFP/FPD) develops and coordinates the Department's position on the foreign policy aspects of domestic farm legislation, international trade policy, and on proposals to promote agricultural exports. It represents or advises the US representatives in international organizations concerned with food policy, such as the FAO, OECD, the International Wheat Council, and the World Food Conference.

DEVELOPMENT COORDINATION COMMITTEE
    c/o Administrator, USAID
    Washington, D.C. 20523

Established in 1975 to advise the President on foreign policies and programs affecting the development of Third World nations. The Committee is concerned with the foreign policy objectives and impacts of American food aid.

INTERNATIONAL DEVELOPMENT COOPERATION AGENCY (IDCA)
    IDCA Planning Office, Rm. 3932
    Department of State
    Washington, D.C. 20523
    (202) 655-4000

    Responsible for establishing overall development assistance policy and for coordinating international development activities supported by the United States. IDCA includes AID, and the Overseas Private Investment Corporation.

GENERAL ACCOUNTING OFFICE (GAO)
    441 G. Street, N.W.
    Washington, D.C. 20548
    (202) 275-2812

    Serves as the investigative arm of the U.S. Congress. Performs independent audits on P.L. 480 operations at home and abroad. Publications: <u>The Monthly List of GAO Reports</u>; <u>Foreign Investment in U.S. Agricultural Land: How it Shapes Up</u> (July, 1979); <u>The World Food Program—How the U.S. Can Help Improve It</u> (May, 1977); and various others listed in this bibliography.

OFFICE OF TECHNOLOGY ASSESSMENT (OTA)
    119 D Street, N.E.
    Washington, D.C. 20510
    (202) 224-8711

    Established in 1972 to assist the United States Congress assess the consequences of American technology. National food policy is one of the seven broad program areas of the OTA. Publications: <u>Emerging Food Marketing Technologies</u> (October 1978); and <u>Organizing and Financing Basic Research to Increase Food Production</u> (June 1977).

PRESIDENTIAL COMMISSION ON WORLD HUNGER (PCWH)
    734 Jackson Place, N.W.
    Washington, D.C. 20006
    (202) 395-3505

    Established in 1978 to develop recommendations for the President of th United States to significantly reduce world hunger and malnutrition and to focus on better and more equitable solutions to hunger with members of Congress, the Administration, and various international organizations. Publications: <u>see</u> Presidential Commission on World Hunger in this bibliography.

U. S. CONGRESS, HOUSE AGRICULTURE COMMITTEE
 1301 Longworth House Office Building
 Washington, D.C. 20515
 (202) 225-2171

 This Committee examines all United States domestic and international food aid programs prior to the allocation of funding for the projects. It has three subcommittees: The Subcommittee on Domestic Marketing, Consumer Relations, and Nutrition; the Subcommittee on Family Farms, Rural Development and Special Studies; and the Subcommittee on Livestock and Grains. Works in conjuncton wtih the U.S. Congress, Senate, Committee on Agriculture, Nutrition and Forestry. Publications: Several recent publications are listed in this bibliography, see U. S. Congress, House Agriculture Committee.

U. S. CONGRESS, HOUSE COMMITTEE ON FOREIGN AFFAIRS
 2170 Rayburn House Office Building
 Washington, D.C. 20515
 (202) 225-5021

 Holds several hearings annually on the subject of international food aid and development. Monitors progress of U.S. food aid programs. Sub-divided into four sub-committees: Subcommittee on Asian and Pacific Affairs; Subcommittee on International Organizations, Subcommittee on Africa; Subcommittee on International Economic Policy and Trade; Subcommittee on Inter-American Affairs. Publications: Foreign Assistance Legislation for Fiscal Year 1980 and 1981 (March 1979); and other documents listed in this bibliography, see U. S. Congress, House Committee on Foreign Affairs.

U. S. CONGRESS, SENATE COMMITTEE ON AGRICULTURE, NUTRITION AND FORESTRY
 322 Russell Senate Office Building
 Washington, D.C. 20510
 (202) 224-2035

 Reviews U. S. international food aid programs before congressional appropriations are made. Three subcommittees monitor and formulate U. S. food and agricultural policies: the Subcommittee on Agricultural Production, Marketing, and Stabilization of Prices; the Subcommittee on Foreign Agricultural Policy; the Subcommittee on Nutrition; and the Subcommittee on Rural Development. Works in conjunction with the U. S. Congress House Agriculture Committee. Publications: Dietary Goals for the United States, Second Edition (1977); and other publications listed in this bibliography, see U. S. Congress, Senate Committee on Agriculture, Nutrition and Forestry.

U. S. CONGRESS, SENATE COMMITTEE ON FOREIGN RELATIONS
4229 Dirksen Senate Office Building
Washington, D.C. 20510
(202) 224-4651

Concerned with the political impact of U. S. international food aid porgrams. It has a Subcommittee on International Economic Policy.

UNITED STATES

Private, State and Voluntary Organizations

AD HOC JEWISH COMMITTEE ON HUNGER
808 West end Avenue, Suite 1004
New York, New York 10025 USA

Increases awareness in the Jewish community about world food problems and their possible solutions.

AFRICARE
1601 Connecticut Avenue, N.W.
Washington, D.C. 20009
(202) 462-3614

Established in 1972, Africare is dedicated to the improvement of the quality of life in rural Africa. It provides short-term food aid and long-range developmental assistance. "Funds donated for relief are used for such things as the purchase of high protein foods, medicines and supplies, powdered milk, blankets, domestic animals and farm implements." Long-term development projects usually focus on water resource development, agriculture and food production, and rural health services. Maintains overseas offices in Niamey, Niger; Bamako, Mali; and Ouagadougou, Upper Volta. Publications: Africare Newsletter (quarterly).

AGRICULTURAL DEVELOPMENT COUNCIL
1290 Avenue of the Americas
New York, New York 10020
(212) 765-3500

Established in 1953 by John D. Rockefeller III to support teaching and research activities related to the problems of agricultural development. Publication: Newsletter (quarterly).

AMERICAN BAPTIST CHURCHES IN THE U.S.A.
    Board of International Ministries
    Valley Forge, Pennsylvania 19481
    (215) 768-2000

    Provides personnel and funds to agricultural development projects at its missions in Zaire, Burma, the Philippines, Haiti, India, and Thailand.

AMERICAN COUNCIL OF VOLUNTARY AGENCIES IN FOREIGN SERVICE, INC.
    225 Park Avenue South
    New York, New York 10003
    (212) 777-5400

    Coordinates the activities of approximately 40 US-based voluntary agencies involved in the provision of food aid and development assistance abroad. The Council operates the Technical Assistance Information Clearing House (TAICH) which makes recent research available and disseminates information to members. TAICH publications include: TAICH News (quarterly); U.S. Non-Profit Organizations in Development Assistance Abroad (1971); A listing of U.S. Non-Profit Organizations in Food Production and Agricultural Assistance Abroad (1974); and A TAICH Bibliography on Development Assistance.

AMERICAN ENTERPRISE INSTITUTE FOR PUBLIC POLICY RESEARCH (AEI)
    1150 17th Street, N.W.
    Washington, D.C. 20036
    (202) 862-5800

    Established in 1943, this agency conducts business-oriented policy research. Food related publications include: World Food Problems and Prospects (1975); and Food Stamps and Nutrition (1975).

AMERICAN FRIENDS SERVICE COMMITTEE (AFSC)
    World Hunger/Development Project
    15 Rutherford Place
    New York, New York 10003
    (212) 777-4600

    Established in 1917, by the Religious Society of Friends (Quakers). The Committee's World Hunger/Development Project is designed to "develop an informed public engaged in an ongoing effort to effect the policies necessary to end the world hunger problem." It conducts training programs and policy briefings to help support effective hunger actions by community and church groups. Publications: World

Hunger Actionletter (monthly, free); ask for free publications list.

ASSOCIATION OF U. S. UNIVERSITY DIRECTORS OF INTERNATIONAL AGRICULTURAL PROGRAMS
c/o International Programs in Agriculture
Purdue University
Lafayette, Indiana 47907
(317) 494-8753

Established in 1964 to promote communication among directors of university-based international agricultural programs in the US. Publication: Annual Report.

BAPTIST WORLD RELIEF
1628 16th Street, N.W.
Washington, D.C.
(202) 265-5027

Raises and disburses funds for the support of agricultural and development projects in developing countries.

BREAD FOR THE WORLD
207 East 16th Street
New York, New York 10003
(212) 260-7000

Established in 1974 as a "Christian citizen's movement on hunger and poverty." Main purpose is to "enlist ordinary citizens to contact their members of congress and other government leaders regarding U. S. policy matters that vitally affect hungry people." Concerns include international food aid policy, and domestic hunger and poverty in the US. Publications: Bread for the World (1975); Bread for the World Newsletter (monthly) and various papers on food policy related topics.

BROOKINGS INSTITUTION
1775 Massachusetts Avenue, N.W.
Washington, D.C. 20036
(202) 797-6000

Established in 1927 to analyze current and emerging public policy problems in the areas of economics, foreign policy, government and the social sciences. Also concerned with international food policy issues. Publications: Rebuilding Grain Reserves: Toward an International System (1976); The Nutrition Factor: Its Role in National Development

(1973); and <u>The Distribution of Farm Subsidies: Who Benefits?</u> (1971).

CARE
   See: Cooperative for American Relief Everywhere.

CATHOLIC RELIEF SERVICES
   1011 First Avenue
   New York, New York 10022
   (212) 838-4700

   "Official overseas relief and development agency of the (Roman) Catholic hierachy of the U.S." Operated as part of the US Catholic Conference, CRS provides financial support of agricultural development and food production activities in developing nations. Projects include the provision of improved agricultural technology (seeds, tools, etc.); construction of wells and irrigation systems; crop storage and food preservation; nutrition education and construction of feeder roads. Major food-related programs are in Morocco, Jordan, Egypt, Tunisia, India, Bangladesh, the Philippines, Indonesia, Chad, Mali, Mauritania, Niger, Senegal, Upper Volta, Ghana, Tanzania, Rwanda, Ethiopia, Guatemala, Dominican Republic, Honduras, El Salvador, Haiti, Bolivia, Chile, Colombia, Peru and Ecuador.

CENTER OF CONCERN
   3700 13th Street, N.E.
   Washington, D.C. 20017
   (202) 635-2757

   Established in 1971 to promote social jutice in the world community at the policymaking level and with the general public. The Center's "Policy and Value Questions in a New International Economic Order" project addresses food policy questions as an issue of social justice within the world community. Publication: <u>Center Focus</u> (bimonthly).

CHRISTIAN CHURCH (Disciples of Christ)
   Division of Overseas Ministries
   222 S. Downey Avenue
   Indianapolis, Indiana 46219
   (317) 353-1491

   Provides financial assistance to agricultural development projects in developing countries of Zaire, Paraguay, and India. Emphasis is placed on water development; experimental work in agriculture; and livestock programs.

CHRISTIAN REFORMED WORLD RELIEF COMMITTEE (CRWRC)
    2850 Kalamazoo Avenue
    Grand Rapids, Michigan 49508
    (616) 241-1691

    Established in 1962, the CRWRC provides financial support for agricultural development projects in six countries including Mexico, the Philippines, Bangladesh, and Nigeria.

CHURCH WOMEN UNITED (CWU)
    475 Riverside Drive, Room 812
    New York, New York 10027
    (212) 870-3048

    Established in 1941 by various Protestant and Catholic women's organizations to "express the ecumenical dimensions of their faith." Financial assistance of food aid is provided for agricultural development porjects in developing countries through existing international food relief agencies such as Church World Service, UNICEF, and various other churches.

CHURCH WORLD SERVICE (CWS)
    475 Riverside Drive
    New York, New York 10027
    (212) 870-2257

    An agency of the National Council of Churches Division of Overseas Ministries. Established in 1946, CWS is the major overseas relief and development unit of the Council. It provides emergency food aid, often in coordination with USDA and USAID, technical assistance and loans to assist agricultural and community development projects abroad. These programs operate in more than 40 countries in Africa, Asia, Latin America, Europe, and the Middle East. CWS maintains over 15 field offices in countries in Africa, South Asia, and Latin America.

COMMITTEE FOR ECONOMIC DEVELOPMENT (CED)
    477 Madison Avenue
    New York, New York 10022
    (212) 688-2063

    Established in 1942 by non-partisan businessmen interested in conducting research and formulating policy. Publication: <u>A New U.S. Farm Policy for Changing World Food Needs</u> (typewritten statement).

CONSORTIUM FOR INTERNATIONAL DEVELOPMENT (CID)
    c/o Utah State University, UMC-35
    Logan, Utah 84322
    (801) 752-4100, ext. 7471

Consortium of six western universities: the Universities of California and Arizona, Colorado State University, Oregon State University, Texas Tech University, and Utah State University. The Consortium seeks to improve agricultural development overseas emphasizing the increase of world food supplies through better soil, water, and plant management. Projects have taken place in Niger, Bolivia, Iran and various other countries.

COOPERATIVE FOR AMERICAN RELIEF EVERYWHERE (CARE)
    660 First Avenue
    New York, New York 10016
    (212) 686-3110

Established in 1945 as a federation of religious, ethnic, labor and other agencies interested in providing food aid, supplies, and other self-help materials to developing countries. CARE is the largest supplier of Title II Food for Peace aid to developing countries. It operates in over 40 developing countries in Asia, Africa, Latin America, and the Middle East. CARE has conducted food aid or food distribution programs in Egypt, Afghanistan, Belize, Kenya, Lesotho, Liberia, Nicaragua, Nigeria, Peru, South Korea, Haiti, Dominican Republic, Ecuador, Guatemala, Honduras, Hong Kong, India, Indonesia, Israel-Gaza, Jordan, Macao, Mali, Niger, Pakistan, Panama, the Philippines, Sierra Leone, Sri Lanka, Tunisia, and Turkey. Publication: <u>World Report</u> (quarterly) and various reports.

CROP, The Community Hunger Appeal of Church World Service
    28606 Phillips Street
    Elkhart, Indiana 46514
    (219) 264-3102

Established in 1947 to raise money and other assistance to be used by Church World Service and other relief agencies in providing emergency food aid and other self-help aid for development projects.

FRIENDS COMMITTEE ON NATIONAL LEGISLATION (FCNL)
    245 Second Street, N.E.
    Washington, D.C. 20002
    (202) 547-4343

Established in 1943 as an autonomous political committee of the Religious Society of Friends (Quakers). It "conducts background research, legislative analysis, and lobbying and advocacy. It conducts legislative research and lobbying to promote policies which will help eradicate hunger in the long run. It calls for an increase in U.S. food aid and admonishes the use of food assistance for war or political purposes. Attempts to favorably impact upon US international and domestic food policies. Publication: FCNL Washington Newsletter (monthly) and various other pamphlets and legislative reports.

HEIFER PROJECT INTERNATIONAL (HPI)
825 W. 3rd
P. O. Box 808
Little Rock, Arkansas 72203
(501) 376-6836

Established in 1944, the HPI provides food assistance to some 90 developing countries in the form of livestock, poultry, or technical assistance to small farmers. Regional officers are located in Plymouth, Massachusetts; Goshen, Indiana; El Monte, California; and Modesto, California. Publication: Sharing Life (quarterly).

INSTITUTE FOR FOOD AND DEVELOPMENT POLICY (IFDP)
2588 Mission Street
San Francisco, California 94110
(415) 648-6090

Established in 1975 by Frances Moore Lappe and Joseph Collins to "try to integrate understanding of all aspects of the food issue, particularly U. S. agriculture, trade, aid, and monetary policies." It is a documentation, research and education center working to identify the root causes of hunger and food problems in the United States and abroad. The IFDP examines the food policies of both governments and corporations and investigates measures which will create social, economic and political structures that ensure food security for all. Publications: Food First: Beyond the Myth of Scarcity (1977); The Aid Debate: Assessing the Impact of Foreign Assistance and the World Bank (1979).

INTERNATIONAL FOOD POLICY RESEARCH INSTITUTE (IFPRI)
1776 Massachusetts Avenue, N.W.
Washington, D.C. 20036
(202) 862-5600

Established in 1976 to "identify and analyze alternative national and international strategies and policies for meeting food needs in the world, with particular emphasis on low-income countries and the poorer groups in those countries. While the research effort is geared to the precise objective of contributing to the reduction of hunger and malnutrition, the factors involved are many and wide-ranging, requiring analysis of underlying processes and extending beyond a narrowly defined food sector. The Institute's research program reflects worldwide interaction with policymakers, administrators and others concerned with increasing food production and with improving the equity of its distribution. Research results published and distributed to officials and others concerned with national and international food and agricultural policy." The IFPRI is a member of the Consultative Group on International Agricultural Research. Publications: IFPRI Report (3/year); and others, see International Food Policy Research Institute in bibliography.

INTERRELIGIOUS TASKFORCE ON U.S. FOOD POLICY
    110 Maryland Avenue, N.E.
    Washington, D.C. 20002
    (202) 543-2800

Coalition of over 20 Protestant, Roman Catholic, and Jewish agencies "who work together to facilitate the witness of the American religious community for a responsible U. S. food policy." Maintains active interests in U. S. food aid (P.L. 480), U. S. economic aid and development assistance to developing nations, U. S. domestic food programs, and U. S. agricultural policy. Publication: IMPACT/Hunger, bimonthly.

IOWA STATE UNIVERSITY
    Center for Agricultural and Economic Development
    East Hall
    Ames, Iowa 50010
    (515) 294-4111

Established in 1957, the Center's research projects focus on development issues, including the role of agriculture in economic development; interrelationships between domestic farm policies and international trade and aid; and international food aid policy. Publications: Several publications are listed in the annotated bibliography section.

LUTHERAN WORLD RELIEF
    360 Park Avenue South
    New York, New York 10010
    (212) 532-6350

    Established in 1945 as an agency of the Lutheran Churches of the U.S. concerned with the promotion of agricultural development in developing countries. Distributes Title II P.L. 480 food aid overseas for the USDA and USAID through food for work programs. The agency has provided emergency food aid to many countries including; Ethiopia, Mauritania, Mozambique, Niger, Sudan, Tanzania, Togo, Bangladesh, India, Viet-Nam, Jordan, Brazil, Chile, and Guatemala.

MASSACHUSETTS INSTITUTE OF TECHNOLOGY (MIT)
    Cambridge, Massachusetts 02139
    (617) 253-1550

    Established in 1956, the Institute is involved in a number of research projects dealing with agricultural development problems.

MENNONITE CENTRAL COMMITTEE (MCC)
    21 S. 12th Street
    Akron, Pennsylvania 17501
    (717) 859-1151

    Established in 1920 as the relief and service agency of North American Mennonite and Brethren in Christ churches. It sponsors a considerable number of agricultural development and food production projects in over 35 countries.

MICHIGAN STATE UNIVERSITY
    Institute of International Agriculture
    113 Agriculture Hall
    East Lansing, Michigan 48823
    (517) 355-0174

    Part of the College of Agriculture. Conducts research in international aspects of agricultural science, food and nutrition, rural development, and natural resources. In 1964, the Institute corroborated with USAID on an extensive study of the U.S. food aid program, Food for Peace. Publications: See annotations in bibliography.

NATIONAL COUNCIL OF CHURCHES OF CHRIST IN THE U.S.A. (NCC)
    475 Riverside Drive
    New York, New York 10027
    (212) 870-2200

Established in 1950 as a federation of 31 Protestant and Eastern Orthodox denominations with a total combined membership of over 41 million. The NCC is concerned with both domestic and international issues of food and development. Those agencies or divisions dealing primarily with issues of international food aid or agricultural development include:

> The Interreligious Foundation for Community Organization (IFCO) - One of its programs. Relief for Africans in Need in the Sahel (RAINS), was engaged in famine relief efforts in the Sahel region of West Africa. The agency contributed directly to the passage of emergency food aid legislation to the Sahel during the 1973-75 period which led to the authorization of millions of dollars of U.S. food aid to the Sahel and the establishment of the USAID long term Sahel Development Program.

> The Division of Overseas Ministries (DOM) - is concerned with the development of international food policy and provides direct emergency relief. It sponsors two agencies which provide international food aid: Church World Service (CWS) and CROP. See separate entries for description of these agencies. DOM also coordinates the activities of the Agricultural Missions --the technical agency for agriculture and rural development.

OVERSEAS DEVELOPMENT COUNCIL (ODC)
    1717 Massachusetts Avenue, N.W.
    Washington, D.C. 20036
    (202) 234-8701

Established in 1969, the ODC attempts to "keep the urgency of the challenges of development before the American public and responsible authorities; to serve as a forum for individual directly concerned with development to share ideas through conferences, seminars, and discussions; to conduct studies of its own on current and emerging problems; and to distribute information and knowledge about development as widely as possible." A major interest of the ODC has been world food policy and its impact on development. Publication: See annotations in this bibliography; publications are available individually or on a subscription basis (list on request).

OXFAM-AMERICA
    302 Columbus Avenue
    Boston, Massachusetts 02116
    (617) 247-3304

Established in 1970 as a development assistance and emergency relief organization which is part of a worldwide network known as OXFAM. OXFAM is an outgrowth of the Oxford Committee for Famine Relief organized in 1942 to aid refugees. The agency funds some agricultural projects in developing countries and works in America to develop greater awareness about hunger and nutrition abroad.

PRESBYTERIAN CHURCH IN THE UNITED STATES (PCUS)
    Taskforce on World Hunger
    341 Ponce de Leon Avenue, N.E.
    Atlanta, Georgia 30308
    (404) 873-1531

    Provides some funding to agricultural development projects overseas. Forum for discussion of food policy issues within the denomination.

PRIVATE AGENCIES COLLABORATING TOGETHER (PACT)
    777 United Nations Plaza
    New York, New York 10017
    (212) 697-6222

    A coalition of independent, voluntary agencies working together to promote a coordinated approach to development planning and the administration of projects overseas. PACT agencies collaborate on issues of international food policy and development. Sponsors agricultural projects operating in Ghana, Kenya, Liberia, the Philippines, Dominican Republic, Ecuador, El Salvador, Honduras, and Nicaragua.

PUBLIC WELFARE FOUNDATION
    2600 Virginia Avenue, N.W.
    Washington, D.C. 20037
    (202) 965-1800

    Provides several grants for agricultural development to Third World countries. Projects emphasize irrigation and the provision of agricultural technical assistance. Operates agricultural projects in Mali, Mauritania, Niger, Brazil, Mexico, Panama, and Peru.

ROCKEFELLER BROTHERS FUND
    1290 Avenue of the Americas
    New York, New York 10020
    (212) 397-4800

    The Fund supports a few agricultural development projects

in developing countries, placing emphasis on their relation to economic systems and the political development of the country.

THE ROCKEFELLER FOUNDATION (RF)
1133 Avenue of the Americas
New York, New York 10036
(212) 869-8500

Established in 1913, the Foundation has been concerned with the improvement of the food supply and the elimination of hunger in the developing countries. It supports 9 international agricultural research institutes sponsored by the Consultative Group on International Agricultural Research. Grants are provided for various agricultural projects in developing countries "to identify strategies for improving the standard of living for small farmers and to increase understanding of the socio-economic aspects of food production and distribution. Publications: RF Illustrated (quarterly); The World Food Situation: A New Initiative (1975); Strategies for Agricultural Education in Developing Countries, and others.

SEVENTH-DAY ADVENTIST WORLD SERVICE
6840 Eastern Avenue, N.W.
Washington, D.C. 20012
(202) 723-0800

Development arm of the General Conference of Seventh-day Adventists. Provides international food assistance to developing countries.

SIERRA CLUB
530 Bush Street
San Francisco, California 94108
(415) 981-8634

Established in 1892, the Sierra Club is a major US conservation foundation. It is also concerned with international food and development policy. Publications: Sierra Club Bulletin (monthly); and National News Report (weekly).

STANFORD UNIVERSITY
Food Research Institute
Stanford, California 94305
(415) 497-3653

Established in 1921, the University is a major teaching and

research facility concerned primarily with economic analysis of international food and development issues. Emphasis is placed on problems of income growth and distribution in developing countries. Publications: <u>Food Research Institute Studies</u> (quarterly); Studies in Commodity Economics and Agriculture Policy series; and various others.

SOUTHERN BAPTIST CONVENTION
    460 James Robertson Parkway
    Nashville, Tennessee 37210
    (615) 244-2495

Concerned with issues of international food relief and world hunger, the Southern Baptist Convention educates its members about social justice issues and raises funds to support agricultural development in developing countries of Latin America, Africa and the Middle East.

SUDAN INTERIOR MISSION, INC.
    Cedar Grove, New Jersey 07009
    (201) 857-1100

Provides agricultural supplies and technical assistance to agricultural development projects in Ethiopia and Niger.

SYNAGOGUE COUNCIL OF AMERICA (SCA)
    432 Park Avenue South
    New York, New York 10016
    (212) 686-8670

Established in 1926 as umbrella organization for Orthodox, Conservative, and Reform Jews in the United States. Promotes Jewish involvement on issues of international food policy and development.

TRANS TECH MANAGEMENT
    P. O. Box 23032
    Sacramento, California
    (916) 421-9382

Consulting agency concerned with food aid and development issues.

TRILATERAL COMMISSION
    North American Office
    345 East 46th Street
    New York, New York 10017
    (212) 661-1180

Established in 1973 and chaired by David Rockefeller. Membership includes over 300 individuals from North America, Western Europe and Japan. It seeks to build consensus among First World policy makers on global issues including the world food problem. Publications: <u>Trialogue</u> 4/year); <u>Industrial Policy and the International Economy</u>; and various others.

UNION OF AMERICAN HEBREW CONGREGATIONS (UAHC)
    838 Fifth Avenue
    New York, New York 10021
    (212) 249-0100

Established in 1873 as the central congregational body of Reform Judaism in the Western Hemisphere. It's Commission on Social Action of Refrorm Judaism is concerned with issues of international food policy.

UNITED METHODIST COMMITTEE ON RELIEF (UMCOR)
    475 Riverside Drive
    New York, New York 10027
    (212) 749-0700

Established in 1940 as the overseas development and relief organization of the United Methodist Church. Promotes issues of international food policy and development to members; raises funds to support agricultural development and food-related activites in Niger, Sudan, Bolivia, Haiti, Honduras, Nicaragua, Peru, Bangladesh, India, Jordan, and Pakistan.

UNITED NATIONS ASSOCIATION OF THE UNITED STATES OF AMERICA
    (UNA-USA)
    300 E. 42nd Street
    New York, New York 10017
    (212) 697-3232

Established by a council of organizations in 1964 which "seeks, through information, education, and research, to strengthen this country's (US) capacity for advancing the ideals of the United Nations." Particularly interested in issues of international food aid, policy and development.

THE UNITED PRESBYTERIAN CHURCH IN THE U.S.A.
    The Program Agency
    475 Riverside Drive
    New York, New York 10027
    (212) 870-2316

Provides financial assistance to agricultural development projects and research institutes in many developing countries, including Kenya, Sudan, Zaire, Zambia, Taiwan, Thailand, India, Nepal, and Guatemala.

UNITED STATES CATHOLIC CONFERENCE (USCC)
1312 Massachusetts Avenue, N.W.
Washington, D.C. 20005
(202) 659-6600

Established in 1919 as the organizing council of the Roman Catholic bishops in the US. Its Office of International Justice and Peace formulates international food policy and carries on projects of legislative and administrative action. International food aid is provided by the USCC Catholic Relief Service (see separate entry).

UNIVERSITY OF CALIFORNIA, BERKELEY
Giannini Foundation of Agricultural Economics
207 Giannini Hall
Berkeley, California 94720
(415) 642-3345

Provides research on agricultural development issues of developing cuntries. Maintains extensive library facilities. Concerned with issues of international food policy.

UNIVERSITY OF CALIFORNIA, DAVIS
Agricultural Economics Department
Davis, California 95616
(916) 752-1514

The Department of Agricultural Economics is internationally renowned. It trains Americans and Third World students to provide agricultural development assistance. Currently involved in a multi-million dollar joint project of the University of California and USDA/USAID providing agricultural and economic assistance to Egypt.

UTAH STATE UNIVERSITY
Office of International Programs
Logan, Utah 84321
(801) 752-4100

Operates agricultural development projects under contract with USAID in various Third World countries including Bolivia, Iran, Cameroon, and Mali.

WORLD HUNGER EDUCATION/ACTION TOGETHER (WHEAT)
475 Riverside Drive, Room 634
New York, New York 10027
(212) 870-2331

A collaborative effort of several Protestant denominations to "mobilize persons concerned about hunger." It is concerned with the formulation of international food policy and works closely with the Interreligious Taskforce on U.S. Food Policy. WHEAT is coordinated by the National Council of Churches but is not a Council program.

WORLD NEIGHBORS (WN)
5116 N. Portland Avenue
Oklahoma City, Oklahoma 73112
(405) 946-3333

Established in 1951, WN provides agricultural development assistance to more than 30 countries in Africa, Latin America, East and South Asia. Projects include improvement of marketing systems for agricultural products; provision of farm implements; seed distibution; and water irrigation. Publication: World Neighbors Newsletter (quarterly).

WORLD VISION INTERNATIONAL (WV)
919 W. Huntington Drive
Monrovia, California 91016
(213) 357-7979

Established in 1950 as an interdenominational Christian organization. It provides food aid to about 100,000 children in more than 39 countries through its relief arm, the World Vision Relief Organization (WVRO). It also provides funding to agricultural development projects in Ethiopia, Kenya, the Gambia, Senegal, Niger, Upper Volta, South Korea, India, the Philippines, Indonesia and Thailand. WV maintains offices in Bangladesh; Brazil; Ethiopia; Hong Kong; India; Indonesia; Kenya; Korea; Philippines and Thailand.

UNITED NATIONS SYSTEM

Multilateral Agencies, and Intergovernmental Organizations

AFRICAN DEVELOPMENT BANK
P. O. Box 1387
Abidjan, Ivory Coast
West Africa

Provides some concessional loans to agricultural development projects in Africa.

AFRO-ASIAN RURAL RECONSTRUCTION ORGANIZATION (AARRO)
C-117/118, Defence Colony
New Delhi 110024, India

Established in 1962 to promote cooperation among member countries (about 24 in Africa and Asia) on problems of welfare, agriculture, hunger and poverty among rural peoples. Funding is provided by affluent states in the region such as Japan, Korea and the League of Arab States. Publications: Rural Reconstruction (journal) and Directory of Professional Organizations of Farmers in Afro-Asian Countries (1968).

ASIAN DEVELOPMENT BANK (ADB)
P. O. Box 789
Manila 2800, Philippines

Established in 1966 as an international development finance institution. It provides loans and grants to agricultural projects; fosters economic growth; and provides technical assistance to some 35 member governments in Asia, Oceania, Europe and North America. Publications: Quarterly Review, Annual Reports.

ASIAN DEVELOPMENT CENTER (ADC)
Philbanking Corp. Building, 11th Floor
Anda Circle, Port Area
Manila, Philippines

Established in 1969, this organization is affiliated with the Asian Parliamentarians' Union (APU). It conducts studies and recommends policies and programs for regional co-operation in various fields, including agriculture.

CARIBBEAN DEVELOPMENT BANK (CDB)
P. O. Box 408
Bridgetown, Barbados
61152

Established in 1969, the CDB provides grants and loans to promote economic growth and development of the 17 countries in the Caribbean, including agricultural projects. Canada and the UK are also members. Publication: Annual Report.

CARIBBEAN FOOD AND NUTRITION INSTITUTE (CFNI)
P. O. Box 140
Kingston 7, Jamaica
78338
  Trinidad Office: University of the West Indies, Campus
    St. Augustine, Trinidad
    662-5510

Established in 1967, the CFNI is composed of 17 English-speaking countries of the Caribbean. CFNI works to improve the food and nutrition situation of the region including training (courses in nutrition, and food and nutrition policy); research, and technical and advisory services. Publications: Cajanus (bimonthly); and other technical papers.

COLOMBO PLAN COUNCIL FOR TECHNICAL CO-OPERATION IN SOUTH AND SOUTH-EAST ASIA
Colombo Plan Bureau, P. O. Box 596
Colombo, Sri Lanka
81813

Established in 1950 by the British Commonwealth to provide aid and technical assistance to underdeveloped countries in Asia and Fiji. Provides grants and loans for agricultural projects and training and experts in agriculture. Japan and the US are also members. Publications: Colombo Plan Newsletter (monthly); Annual Report.

COMMONWEALTH AGRICULTURAL BUREAUX (CAB)
Farnham House, Farnham Royal
Slough SL2 3BN, England
Common 2281

Established by the Commonwealth to provide a scientific information service for agricultural research workers. CAB is composed of 4 institutes and 11 bureaus which provide information on a wide range of agriculture and related fields. CAB offers many services, among them: The International Food Information Service which monitors the food situation and provides computer search service; the Commonwealth Bureau of Agricultural Economics; and the Commonwealth Bureau of Nutrition. Publications: World Agricultural Economics and Rural Sociology Abstracts (monthly); Annotated Bibliographies (list of subjects available); Nutrition Abstracts and Reviews (monthly); Food and Technology Abstracts (monthly); and a variety of other publications.

CONSULTATIVE GROUP ON INTERNATIONAL AGRICULTURAL RESEARCH (CGIAR)
c/o World Bank
1818 H Street, N.W.
Washington, D.C. 20433
(202) 477-2747

Provides funding to several international institutes for agricultural research including the International Rice Research Institute (IRRI), International Maize and Wheat Improvement Center (CIMMYT) International Center of Tropical Agriculture (CIAT), International Crops Institute for the Semi-Arid Tropics (ICRISAT), International Potato Center (CIP), International Board for Plant Genetic Resources (IBPGR), International Laboratory for Research on Animal Diseases (ILRAD), and the International Livestock Center for Africa (ILCA). The Group is composed of members of the World Bank, FAO, UNDP, donor governments, regional development banks, the Commission of the European Communities, the Ford, Kellogg, and Rockefeller Foundations, and the International Development Research Center of Canada.

CONSULTATIVE GROUP ON FOOD PRODUCTION AND INVESTMENT IN DEVELOPING COUNTRIES (CGFPI)
1818 H Street, N.W.
Washington, D.C. 20433
(202) 477-2041

Established in 1975, this agency is jointly administered by the FAO, UNDP and World Bank. It encourages larger external resource flows for food production in developing countries and coorinates donor activities.

ECONOMIC AND SOCIAL COMMISSION FOR ASIA AND THE PACIFIC (ESCAP)
United Nations Building
Rajdamnern Avenue
Bangkok, Thailand

Includes a joint ESCAP/FAO Agriculture Division. It functions to improve agricultural plans and policies of countries in this regional grouping and to promote regional agricultural cooperation. Responsible to the United Nations Economic and Social Council (ECOSOC), United Nations, New York, New York, 10017.

ECONOMIC COMMISSION FOR AFRICA (ECA)
P. O. Box 3001
Addis Ababa, Ethiopia

This agency reports directly to the United Nations Economic and Social Council (ECOSOC). It addresses problems of food and agricultural development in Africa in addition to other issues of regional cooperation.

ECONOMIC COMMISSION FOR EUROPE (ECE)
Palais des Nations
1211 Geneva 10, Switzerland

The Committee on Agricultural Problems addresses questions of food policy and food assistance. The agency is responsible to the United Nations Economic and Social Council (ECOSOC), United Nations, New York, New York, 10017.

ECONOMIC COMMISSION FOR LATIN AMERICA (ECLA)
Avenida Dag Hammarsjold, Vitacura
Santiago, Chile

Responsible to the United Nations Economic and Social Council (ECOSOC), this agency includes a Joint ECLA/FAO Agriculture Division concerned with the improvement of agricultural plans and policies of countries in the region.

EUROPEAN COMMUNITIES
Commission of the European Communities
200, rue de la Loi
1049 Brussels, Belgium
735-00-40

Members of the European Communities include Belgium, Federal Republic of Germany, France, Italy, Luxembourg, Netherlands, Denmark, Ireland, and United Kingdom. The EC's European Development Fund (EDF) gives non-repayable grants to countries for various purposes, including agricultural development. In 1974, 44 % of its disbursements were for food aid. The EC maintains offices in each member country and information offices in Chile, Greece, Japan, Switzerland and Turkey. Publications: <u>Memorandum on Food Aid Policy of the European Economic Commission: Communication from the Commission to the Council</u> (1974); <u>Bulletin of the European Communities</u> (monthly); and various studies, reports and other publications.

FOOD AND AGRICULTURE ORGANIZATION (FAO)
Via delle Terme di Caracalla
00100 Rome, Italy
    Liaison Office for North America:
            1776 F Street, N.W.
            Washington, D.C. 20437
            (202) 634-6200

The FAO is a specialized agency of the United Nations. Its constitution became effective October 16, 1945. FAO's main function is to raise nutrition levels and living standards; to secure improvement in production and distribution of food and agricultural products; to monitor the world food situation; and to better the conditions of rural populations. It is governed by a Conference of 144 United Nations Member states, which meets in odd-numbered years; and a 34 member Council. Major committees include: Committee on Commodity Problems; Subcommittee on Surplus Disposal, Committee on Fisheries; Committee on Agriculture, Committee on World Food Security; European Commission on Agriculture; Regional Commission on Animal Production and Health in Africa; Regional Commission on Agricultural Extension for Asia and the Far East; Caribbean Plant Protection Commission; Near East Commission on Agricultural Planning; and a joint FAO/WHO Regional Food and Nutrition Commission for Africa; FAO/Fertilizer Industry Advisory Committee of Experts; Joint FAO/UNICEF Policy Committee; FAO/WHO Committee of Experts on Nutrition; and an Advisory Committee of Experts on Marine Resources and Research.

In addition, the FAO provides technical and financial assistance and participates in the Consultative Group on International Agricultural Research and the Consultative Group on Food Production and Investment in Developing Countries. Publications: A free list of FAO publications may be obtained from UNIPUB, Inc., Box 433, Murray Hill Station, NY, NY 10016. Selected publications include: _FAO Books in Print_ (annually); _Ceres: FAO Review on Development_ (bimonthly); _The State of Food and Agriculture_ (annually;) _Monthly Bulletin of Agricultural Economics and Statistics; Production Yearbook; Trade Yearbook; FAO Commodity Review and Outlook; Food Aid: A Selective Annotated Bibliography on Food Utilization for Economic Development (1964); Food and Nutrition: A Quarterly Review Devoted to World Development in Food Policies and Nutrition_; and _Food and Agricultural Legislation_ (quarterly). The FAO maintains regional offices in Ghana, United States, Thailand, Egypt, and Chile.

GENERAL AGREEMENT ON TARIFFS AND TRADE (GATT)
154 Rue de Lausanne
1211 Geneva 21, Switzerland
    US Liaison Office: GATT
                            United Nations
                            New York, New York 10017
                            (212) 754-1234

Established in 1947, GATT is the main trade policy negotiating forum for developed market economies, including negotiations on food products. Publications: _International_

Trade (annual); GATT Activities (annual); and GATT Studies in International Trade series.

INTER-AMERICAN DEVELOPMENT BANK (IDB)
    808 17th Street, N.W.
    Washington, D.C. 20577
    (202) 634-8000

The IDB provides financial and technical assistance to economic and social development in Latin America. Priority is given to agricultural development projects. The IDB was established in 1959. Publications: Economic and Social Progress in Latin America (annual report); monthly newsletter; free upon request.

INTER-AMERICAN INSTITUTE OF AGRICULTURAL SCIENCES (IICA)
    Apartado 55-Coronado
    Provincia de San Jose, Costa Rica
        US Liaison Office: 1889 F Street, N.W.
                              Washington, D.C. 20006
                              (202) 789-3767

Specialized agency on agriculture of the Organization for American States (OAS) established in 1942.

INTERNATIONAL BANK FOR RECONSTRUCTION AND DEVELOPMENT (IBRD) (World Bank)
    1818 H. Street, N.W.
    Washington, D.C. 20433
    (202) 477-1234

Established in 1944, the World Bank and its affiliates, the International Development Association (IDA), and the International Finacne Corporation (IFC), provide reconstruction and development assistance to its 127 Member countries. The World Bank's loan emphasis is shifting to the funding of agricultural development projects, especially comprehensive rural development programs aimed at smaller farmers and increased rural standards of living. The Bank participates in the Consultative Group on International Agricultural Research and the Consultative Group on Food Production and Investment in Developing Countries.

The World Bank maintains regional offices in France, England, Kenya, Nigeria, Ivory Coast, Sudan, Bangladesh, Afghanistan, Cameroon, Colombia, Ethiopia, Ghana, India, Indonesia, Nepal, Pakistan, Tanzania, Thailand, Upper Volta, Venezuela, Zaire and Zambia. Publications: Annual Report, Quarterly financial statements, World Bank Paper series, World Bank Atlas: Population, Per Capita Product, and Growth Rates (1975); Report (bimonthly newsletter, free); World Development Report (yearly, $3.50) and others. Free list of publications available upon request.

INTERNATIONAL FUND FOR AGRICULTURAL DEVELOPMENT (IFAD)
Via del Serafico 107
EUR 00142
Rome, ITALY
    New York Liaison Office: United Nations
                                           Suite 3255
                                           New York, New York 10017
                                           (212) 754-5506

Established in 1974 by the World Food Conference. The IFAD began operating in 1977. It provides grants and loans to stimulate food production, reduce malnutrition, and improve food distribution system in underdeveloped countries. Funding is usually provided on a concessional basis, in the form of donations or soft loans. IFAD works through pre-established agencies such as the World Bank, FAO, UNDP, and regional development banks. IFAD is governed by an Executive Board composed of 6 representatives from developed countries, 6 from developing contributing (OPEC) countries, and 6 from developing recipient countries.

INTERNATIONAL WHEAT COUNCIL
Haymarket House
28 Haymarket
London SWIY 4SS, United Kingdom

Established in 1947, the International Wheat Council is the main agency for negotiating international wheat agreements. More than 60 countries participate in the negotiations.

ORGANIZATION OF AMERICAN STATES (OAS)
19th and Constitution Avenue, N.W.
Washington, D.C. 20006 USA
(202) 789-3000

Established in 1890, the OAS initiates and funds development projects. Subsidiary bodies which deal with food problems are the Inter-American Committee for Agricultural Development (CIDA) (1725 Eye Street, N.W., Washington, D.C. 20006) and the Inter-American Institute of Agricultural Sciences (IICA) (see separate entry). CIDA is concerned with filling in gaps of information and identifying bottlenecks that obstruct Latin American agricultural development. IICA focuses on strengthening agricultural educational institutions. Publications: Americas (monthly); Report of the Secretary General (annual); and various conference and technical documents.

ORGANIZATION FOR ECONOMIC COOPERATION AND DEVELOPMENT (OECD)
2 Rue Andre Pascal
75775 Paris 16, France
524.81.67
    Publications and Information Center:
                      1750 Pennsylvania Avenue N.W.
                      Washington, D.C. 20006 USA
                      (202) 724-1857

Established in 1960, the main function of the OECD is to promote international trade and investment. OECD members include 24 industrialized nations with market economies which account for about 90% of total official and private flows from all sources (both bilateral and multilateral). Member countries are: Australia, Austria, Belgium, Canada Denmark, Finland, France, Federal Republic of Germany, Greece, Iceland, Ireland, Italy, Japan, Luxembourg, Netherlands, New Zealand, Norway, Portugal, Spain, Sweden, Switzerland, Turkey, United Kingdom, USA. The OECD Development Assistance Committee (DAC), the Committee for Agriculture, and the Directorate for Agriculture and Food are responsible for: 1) regularly assessing the short-, medium-, and long-term outlook for demand and supply of food in the world, with particular emphasis on the policy implications on the agricultural, trade, and aid policies of OECD countries; 2) regularly assessing member countries' food and agriculture policies; 3) assessing farm organization, food processing and marketing developments; 4) analyzing the relationship between agriculture and economic development; 5) analyzing the food problems of the developing world; and 6) monitoring the effectiveness of DAC food aid programs in underdeveloped countries. Publications: OECD publishes a large number of documents; many pertinent titles are listed in the annotated bibliography section of this book.

ORGANIZATION OF THE PETROLEUM EXPORTING COUNTRIES (OPEC)
Dr. Karl Lueger - Ring 10
1010 Vienna, Austria
63-97-80
    US Liaison Office: Kuwait Embassy
                         2940 Tilden Street N.W.
                         Washington, D.C. 20008
                         (202) 966-0702

Established in 1962, the major function of OPEC is the unification of oil policies of member countries, namely Algeria, Libya, Venezuela, Abu Dhabi (United Arab Emirates), Indonesia, Iran, Iraq, Kuwait, Qatar, Saudia Arabia, and Nigeria. The OPEC Special Fund contributed $400 million to the UN International Fund for Agricultural Development (IFAD) making it a major contributor. OPEC may become a significant agricultural development contributor in the future.

PROTEIN-CALORIE ADVISORY GROUP OF THE UNITED NATIONS SYSTEM (PAG)
866 United Nations Plaza, Room 606
New York, N.Y. 10017

Sponsored by FAO, WHO, UNICEF, the World Bank and the UN, this interdisciplinary group advises the United Nations on technical, economic, educational, social, and other aspects of global malnutrition problems. Publication: PAG Bulletin (quarterly).

UNITED NATIONS CHILDRENS FUND (UNICEF)
866 UN Plaza
New York, New York 10017
(212) 754-7845

This agency, established in 1946, is primarily concerned with improving the life of children in developing countries. It advises on food and nutrition policies; trains health and nutrition personnel; supports village technology for improved food production and storage systems; and provides supplies and equipment. It has regional offices in Zambia, Brazzaville, Uganda, France, Senegal, Thailand, Nigeria, Philippines, Lebanon, India, Colombia, Mexico, Peru, Chile and Guatemala. Publications: UNICEF News (quarterly) and other pamphlets and reports.

UNITED NATIONS CONFERENCE ON TRADE AND DEVELOPMENT (UNCTAD)
Palais des Nations
1211 Geneva 10, Switzerland
    US Liaison Office: United Nations
                                  New York, New York 10017
                                  (212) 754-6893

Established in 1964 to coordinate policies to accelerate the economic and social development of developing countries. UNCTAD is the primary economic forum for the Third and Fourth Worlds. Publications list available upon request from the New York office.

UNITED NATIONS DEVELOPMENT PROGRAM (UNDP)
   1 United Nations Plaza
   New York, New York 10017
   (212) 754-4790
        UNDP Liaison Office: 2101 L St., N.W., Suite 209
                                           Washington, D.C. 20037
                                           (202) 296-5074

Established in 1965, this agency has major responsibility for coordinating the work of 22 UN agencies in specialized technical services and pre-investment studies for pilot production facilities in industry and agriculture. About 30% of UNDP expenditures focus on agriculture, forestry, and fisheries. Since UNDP is largely a financing and monitoring organization, its projects are generally carried out by other international agencies including the United Nations, FAO, UNESCO, WHO, World Bank, WMO, World Food Program, UNICEF, and the Inter-American, African, and Asian Development Banks. UNDP participates in the Consultative Group in International Agricultural Research and the Consultative Group on Food Production and Investment in Developing Countries (both World Bank/FAO groups). Publications: <u>Commitment</u> (quarterly); <u>Business Bulletin</u> (monthly); <u>Action UNDP</u> (bimonthly); <u>UNDP Compendium of Approved Projects</u> (annual). Free list of publications and films available.

UNITED NATIONS HIGH COMMISSIONER FOR REFUGEES (UNHCR)
   Palais des Nations
   1211 Geneva 10, Switzerland
   34-60-11

Established in 1951, this agency provides emergency relief, including food aid from the World Food Programme, to refugees. Refugees from Africa have received the bulk of UNHCR food aid in recent years.

UNITED NATIONS INSTITUTE FOR TRAINING AND RESEARCH (UNITAR)
   801 United Nations Plaza
   New York, New York 10017
   (212) 754-1234

Main body in the United Nations responsible for research and training, including those related to the world food situation. Publications: <u>Important for the Future</u> (5 times a year) and other reports.

WORLD FOOD COUNCIL
Via delle Terme di Caracalla
00100 Rome, Italy

New York Liaison Office: United Nations
Suite 3255
New York, New York 10017
(212) 754-5506

Established in 1975, the World Food Council is responsible for monitoring and implementing resolutions of the World Food Conferene (Rome, November 1974). It functions as a "coordinating mechanism to provide overall, integrated and continuing attention for the successful coordination and follow-up of policies concerning food production, nutrition, food security, food trade and food aid, as well as other related matters, by all the agencies of the United Nations system." It consists of 36 Member states selected by the General Assembly. Publications: Press releases and UN documents.

WORLD FOOD PROGRAMME (WFP)
Via delle Terme de Caracalla
00100 Rome, Italy
New York Laison Office: United Nations
New York, New York 10017
(212) 754-8364

A joint program of the United Nations and FAO. This agency was established in 1961 to provide multilateral food aid to developing countries. It also provides money and technical assistance. Food aid is generally provided in the form of "Food for Work". Nevertheless, substantial food aid is provided for emergency relief in the case of natural disasters and to refugees. Care is taken to determine "whether there is any danger that the arrival of food may have a harmful, dampening effect on local food production or the country's agricultural trade." Emphasis is placed on self-help, rural development and the promotion of balanced, adequate diets. The World Food Programme is administered by the FAO and supervised by a 24 member Intergovernmental Committee (IGC) composed of U.N. and FAO Member States. Publications: <u>Ten Years of Development Aid. 1963-1972</u>; <u>World Food Programme News</u> (newsletter, free from FAO Liaison Office.); <u>World Food Program: A Story of Multilateral Aid</u> (revised periodically); <u>Food Aid to Education and Training</u> (1973); and <u>Food Aid and Employment</u> (1973).

WORLD HEALTH ORGANIZATION (WHO)
20 Avenue Appia
1211, Geneva, Switzerland
US Liaison Office: United Nations
Room 2245
New York, New York   10017
(212) 754-1234
Regional Office for the Americas:
525 23rd Street, N.W.
Washington, D.C.   20037
(202) 331-5403

Established in 1946, WHO is governed by the annual World Health Assembly and a 24 member Executive Board. WHO's major purpose is "the attainment of all peoples of the highest possible level of health." It facilitates adoption of national food and nutrition policies; conducts national nutrition surveys and monitors health centers in developing countries; trains nutritional professionals; identifies famine conditions and malnutrition; and provides medical response. WHO regional offices are located in Congo, the United States, Egypt, Denmark, India, and the Philippines. Publications: World Health (bimonthly); WHO Chronicle (monthly); Bulletin of the World Health Organization (2 vols. per year); International Digest of Health Legislation (quarterly); World Health Statistics Report (monthly); and World Health Statistics Annual.

SUBJECT INDEX

AFGHANISTAN
    363, 384, 409, 410, 412, 416, 417

AFRICA
    69, 70, 108, 115, 142, 143, 147, 165, 227, 232, 272, 301, 304, 308, 311, 314, 317, 400

AGENCY FOR INTERNATIONAL DEVELOPMENT (AID)
    165, 232, 262

AGRARIAN REFORM
    163, 172

AGRICULTURAL DEVELOPMENT
    8, 9, 11, 18, 20, 31, 43, 46, 48, 55, 56, 58, 61, 62, 66, 71, 75, 77, 83, 85, 96, 100, 102, 107, 114, 119, 139, 142, 146, 156, 170, 201, 226, 234, 235, 236, 254, 262, 264, 268, 276, 285, 292, 299, 424, 429, 439, 443

AGRICULTURAL EXPORTS
    89, 144, 245, 361, 409-418

AGRICULTURAL INCENTIVES
    286

AGRICULTURAL POLICY
    69, 72, 122, 261
    of developed countries
        50, 82, 97, 98, 103-4, 126, 128, 129, 157, 175-205, 209, 210-214, 217, 264
    of developing countries
        8, 27, 46, 56-7, 86, 105, 113, 125, 128, 137, 142-3, 160, 163, 209, 290

AGRICULTURAL PRODUCTION
    See food production
    2, 3, 27, 56, 151, 241, 282

AGRICULTURAL TRADE
    12, 18, 88, 167, 287, 333, 361, 408, 424

ALGERIA
    204

ARGENTINA
    56, 58, 161, 204, 220

ASIA
    69, 70, 115, 119, 226, 227, 272, 301, 319, 327

AUSTRALIA
    175, 220

AUSTRIA
    176

BAHRAIN
    51

BALANCE OF PAYMENTS
    101, 105, 294

BANGLADESH
    5, 33, 244, 263, 319, 327, 354, 363, 366, 418

BELGIUM
    177

BENIN
    42

BIAFRA
    263

BOLIVIA
    26, 410, 412, 413, 416

BOTSWANA
    272, 273, 274, 439

BRAZIL
    27, 58, 93, 99, 100, 290, 291, 410, 412, 414

CAMBODIA
    now called Kampuchea
    222, 345, 348, 360, 384, 417, 418

CAMEROON
    304

CANADA
    36, 144, 164, 178, 210, 220, 269, 426

CARIBBEAN
    400

CENTRAL AFRICAN REPUBLIC
    304

CEYLON
    30, 410

CHAD
    304

CHILE
    58, 59, 162, 363, 365, 369, 410
    412, 418

CHINA
    11, 22, 108, 113, 137, 171, 283,
    285, 286, 333

COLOMBIA
    30, 47, 72, 88, 100, 267, 270,
    410, 412, 429

COLOMBO PLAN
    207

COMMODITY CREDIT CORPORATION (CCC)
    359, 361

COMMON AGRICULTURAL POLICY (CAP)
    127, 214, 233, 278

CONGO
    See Zaire

CONSULTATIVE GROUP FOR FOOD PRODUCTION
AND INVESTMENT (CGFPI)
    276

CUBA
    387

CZECHOSLOVAKIA
    373, 421

DAHOMEY
    304

DENMARK
    82, 108, 179

DEPENDENCY
    17, 23, 27, 83, 102, 122,
    123, 135, 227, 237, 292

DEVELOPING NATIONS
    18, 31, 34, 35, 36, 38, 49
    53, 68, 73, 75, 81, 83, 90
    115, 122, 126, 128, 136,
    138, 150, 158, 215, 216,
    227, 231, 236, 240, 252,
    257, 276, 284, 295, 321,
    356

DEVELOPMENT PLANS
    1, 8, 29, 105, 151, 204,
    262, 374, 421

DOMINICA
    353

DOMINICAN REPUBLIC
    30, 353, 384, 410, 412,
    413, 415, 416

DROUGHT
    15, 304, 311

DUAL PRICING
    5

ECONOMIC DEVELOPMENT
    (See food aid and development,
    agricultural development)
    111, 117, 151, 170, 235,
    236, 239, 241, 254, 264,
    268

ECUADOR
    416

EGYPT
    7, 281, 305, 318, 363, 366
    369, 418, 439

ETHIOPIA
    262, 263, 268, 304, 312, 363

-168-

EUROPEAN ECONOMIC COMMUNITY
   95, 122, 123, 126, 134, 140, 144,
   157, 200, 233, 278, 365, 425

FAR EAST
   69, 70

FERTILIZER
   5, 16, 148, 284

FINLAND
   180, 382

FOOD
   and nutrition policy
      2, 96, 217, 229, 241, 428
   and politics
      91, 108, 164, 222, 261, 268,
      279, 280
   as political weapon
      41, 83, 84, 102, 114, 261, 423

FOOD AID
   1, 2, 4, 7, 12, 14, 15, 16, 21,
   24, 25, 26, 32, 33, 34, 35, 36,
   37, 41, 48, 49, 53, 55, 63, 64,
   65, 67, 68, 71, 72, 73, 74, 78,
   79, 81, 84, 90, 93, 94, 95, 100,
   102, 112, 114, 115, 117, 118, 123,
   124, 130, 134, 135, 136, 138,
   139, 144, 146, 150, 151, 152,
   153, 154, 160, 162, 165, 202,
   206, 221, 222, 236, 242, 251,
   259, 263, 265, 267, 276, 297,
   304, 321, 326, 349, 352, 425,
   440
   administration
      4, 12, 35, 67, 71, 73, 236, 243,
      307, 308, 320, 341, 403, 411, 429
   and agricultural production
      3, 4, 7, 33, 37, 88, 93, 151, 160,
      239, 242, 243-4, 253, 257, 260,
      266-7, 272-3, 302, 341, 405, 440
   and balance of payments
      4, 25, 71, 78, 112, 341, 363, 381,
      409, 412, 414, 416, 417, 431
   and commercial trade
      12, 25, 72, 240, 247, 273
   and debt service
      215, 282
   and dependence
      20, 100, 102, 135, 172, 247, 282,
      292, 302
   and development
      1, 4, 16, 25, 39, 55, 64-5
      67, 73, 94, 105, 135, 151,
      201, 203, 207, 208, 232, 236,
      239, 243, 256, 258, 260, 267,
      270-2, 280, 294, 302, 316,
      327, 328, 341, 347, 358, 364,
      393, 409, 411, 414, 426, 429,
      436, 440-442.
   and education
      64, 173, 274, 441
   and employment
      173, 271, 282, 381, 436
   and food reserves
      130, 138, 169, 238, 271
   and foreign policy
      79, 231, 246, 278, 341, 347
   and legal controls
      12, 25, 32
   and market development
      78-9, 114, 158, 259, 271,
      292, 344, 358, 375, 377, 385,
      390, 391, 392, 411-414
   and nutrition
      30, 152, 247, 258, 260, 274,
      399, 433, 441
   and politics
      32, 81, 84, 105, 114, 261,
      264, 281, 288, 445
   and price policy
      4, 228, 230 266
   consumption
      16
   costs
      221
   counterpart funds
      67, 76, 88, 134, 243, 267
   disincentive effect
      7, 15, 33, 40, 57, 117, 118
      124, 149, 250, 253, 255,
      267, 277, 433
   distribution
      16, 25, 96, 205, 206, 230,
      243, 260
   donors
      67, 94, 160, 221, 243, 244,
      405, 431
   emergency donations
      16, 203, 282, 312, 340, 348,
      354, 360, 369, 414, 442
   exports
      14, 233, 381

feeding programs
    153, 154, 272, 274
inflationary effects
    258
legislation
    110, 288, 313, 320, 332, 334,
    342, 362, 363, 368, 369, 375,
    390, 392, 404, 409, 412
management
    33, 67, 94, 206, 271, 347
military uses
    172, 345
multilateral
    60-75, 206, 255, 261, 278, 357,
    399, 406, 424
negotiations
    67, 339, 398, 403
planning and programming
    30, 94, 135, 205, 232, 243, 278,
    341, 356, 363, 370, 375, 376,
    387, 407, 413, 431, 438
policy
    4, 21, 65, 67, 73, 130, 134, 151,
    160, 202, 203, 205, 209, 215,
    260, 265, 271, 272-3, 278, 282,
    292, 331, 341, 385, 400, 405
price effects
    130, 260, 273, 277, 282
projects
    3, 16, 73, 256, 272, 273, 382,
    386
recipients
    67, 84, 94, 124, 130, 134, 160,
    221, 242-44, 248, 257, 267, 282,
    327, 341, 429
self-help activities
    258, 363, 369, 379, 409, 410,
    411, 412-418
supply
    1, 243, 244
utilization
    1, 55, 71, 81, 84, 105, 112, 346,
    369, 375
versus financial assistance
    206, 207, 240, 243, 273

FOOD AID CONVENTION
    104, 220, 293, 294, 363, 393,
    399, 415, 416, 417

FOOD AND AGRICULTURE ACT
    337

FOOD AND AGRICULTURE ORGANIZATION
(FAO)
    60-75, 267, 406

FOOD DISTRIBUTION
    17, 20, 138, 139, 145, 218,
    270, 419, 434

FOOD FOR PEACE PROGRAM
    See Public Law 480
    26, 49, 106, 112, 144, 171,
    288, 334, 336, 363, 369,
    370, 371, 372, 377, 378,
    389, 390, 401, 445

FOOD FOR WORK
    30, 33, 39, 94, 152, 244,
    260, 282, 363, 369, 442

FOODGRAIN
    105, 116, 117, 171
    imports
        33, 141
    supply and distribution
        5, 250, 433

FOOD IMPORTS
    5, 15, 27, 46, 47, 52, 72,
    88, 102, 115, 118, 136, 167
    215, 228, 258, 292, 294,
    419, 422

FOOD MANAGEMENT
    (see food aid management)
    5, 17, 87

FOOD MARKETING
    216

FOOD POLICY
    see food and nutrition policy
    60, 61, 65-66, 68-9, 91,
    102, 104, 116, 120, 122-3,
    125, 237, 261
    of developed countries
        13, 17, 19, 20, 23, 25, 28,
        38, 48, 89, 92, 95, 97, 98,
        103-4, 111, 140, 150, 155,
        165, 167, 219, 223, 224, 231,
        238, 240, 265, 271, 279-80,
        282, 289, 315, 316, 344, 355,
        392, 395, 408, 422, 424-5, 42
        434, 443, 444, 445

of developing countries
5, 22, 29, 51-52, 59, 62, 83, 96,
101, 109-110, 145, 171, 283, 285,
286, 421, 432

FOOD POWER
36, 84, 423

FOOD PRODUCTION
11, 18, 20, 68, 88, 102, 111, 121,
138, 147, 170, 203, 215, 240, 241,
286, 295, 312, 314, 349, 356, 399,
400, 419, 427, 434
policy
9, 54, 145, 168, 228, 284

FOOD RESERVES
see grain reserves, food aid and
food reserves
24, 34, 36, 203, 240, 281, 343,
362, 364

FOOD SECURITY
6, 63, 68, 77, 103, 138, 203, 261,
265, 293, 343, 349, 393, 425

FOOD SECURITY ACT
306, 310

FOOD SECURITY RESERVE
104

FOOD SELF-SUFFICIENCY
17, 52, 70, 86, 92, 101, 102, 109,
114, 138, 139, 147, 249, 271, 291,
293, 373, 399, 422

FOOD STOCKPILING
see food reserves

FOOD STUDY GROUP
95

FOOD SUBSIDY
15, 82, 111

FOOD SUPPLY
68, 71, 75, 92, 96, 103, 150, 167,
399

FOOD SURPLUS
39, 57, 65, 72

FOOD SYSTEM
5

FOREIGN POLICY
77
see food aid and foreign policy

FRANCE
108, 157, 181, 210

GAMBIA
304

GAZA
305

GERMANY
182, 210, 244

GHANA
30, 87, 304, 409, 410, 412
413, 414, 415, 416

GRAIN
41, 374
shortage
16
policy
330, 397

GRAIN RESERVES
see food reserves
63, 104, 121, 169, 218, 224,
238, 289, 306, 310, 325,
326, 335, 337, 394, 396,
399

GREAT BRITAIN
see United Kingdom

GREECE
37, 183

GREEN REVOLUTION
41, 241

GUATEMALA
302

GUINEA
296, 304, 363, 369, 384,
410, 412

GUYANA
410, 412

HAITI
302, 363

HONDURAS
297

ICELAND
184, 409, 410, 412

INCOME DISTRIBUTION
231, 250, 261

INDIA
7, 10, 11, 35, 72, 85, 105, 117,
148, 149, 151, 160, 168, 173,
204, 228, 230, 250, 252, 253,
257, 258, 263, 267, 270, 319,
327, 363, 366, 369, 379, 383,
384, 386, 409, 410, 412-415,
429

INDONESIA
30, 244, 319, 363, 384, 386, 409,
410, 412, 413, 415, 417

INTERNATIONAL COCOA AGREEMENT
131

INTERNATIONAL COFFEE AGREEMENT
132

INTERNATIONAL DEVELOPMENT AND FOOD ASSISTANCE ACT
162, 303, 322, 323, 324, 329,
339

INTERNATIONAL EMERGENCY WHEAT RESERVE
104, 326

INTERNATIONAL FOOD POLICY RESEARCH INSTITUTE
5

INTERNATIONAL FOOD POLITICS RESEARCH GROUP
102

INTERNATIONAL FUND FOR AGRICULTURAL DEVELOPMENT
136, 295

INTERNATIONAL SUGAR AGREEMENT
133

INTERNATIONAL WHEAT AGREEMENT
63, 104, 238, 293, 362-3,
393

IRAN
108, 413

IRAQ
51

IRELAND
185

ISRAEL
35, 72, 160, 270, 363, 369,
383, 409, 410, 412, 429

ITALY
101, 186

IVORY COAST
42, 166, 304

JAMAICA
363

JAPAN
72, 92, 129, 144, 174, 187,
210, 237, 425

JORDAN
305, 363, 369, 410, 412,
416

KAMPUCHEA
see Cambodia

KENYA
107, 204, 304, 308

KERALA
96

KOREA
see South Korea
287, 363, 369, 384, 409,
410, 412, 413, 414

KORRY REPORT
    165

KUWAIT
    51

LAND REFORM
    129, 168, 268

LAND TENURE
    8, 31, 56, 59, 170

LATIN AMERICA
    35, 58, 100, 234, 272, 292, 400

LATIN AMERICAN FREE TRADE ASSOCIATION
    100

LEBANON
    386

LESOTHO
    272, 273, 439

LIBERIA
    410, 412

LIVESTOCK PRODUCTION
    72, 170

LUXEMBURG
    188

MALAWI
    43

MALAYSIA
    30, 204

MALI
    15, 304, 439

MATERNAL/CHILD HEALTH PROGRAMS
    30, 272

MAURITANIA
    15, 304

MEXICO
    58, 204

MOROCCO
    30, 86, 204, 386, 409, 410, 412, 413, 415, 416

MULTINATIONAL CORPORATIONS
    9, 41

MUTUAL SECURITY PROGRAM
    207

NEAR EAST
    69

NEO-COLONIALISM
    102

NEPAL
    319

NETHERLANDS
    189

NEW ZEALAND
    190, 210

NIGER
    15, 16, 42, 304

NIGERIA
    54, 62, 304

NORDIC COUNTRIES
    95

NORWAY
    19, 191, 210, 229, 428

NUTRITION POLICY
    see food and nutrition policy

NUTRITIONAL STATUS
    5

OMAN
    51

ORGANIZATION FOR ECONOMIC COOPERATION AND DEVELOPMENT
    94, 176-216, 243

ORGANIZATION OF PETROLEUM EXPORTING COUNTRIES (OPEC)
    136

PAKISTAN
    7, 72, 108, 151, 160, 244, 263, 319, 327, 354, 363, 367, 369, 384, 386, 409, 410, 412, 416, 417, 418, 429

PARAGUAY
    8, 384, 410, 412, 413

PERU
    58, 94, 100, 204

PHILIPPINES
    30, 119, 204, 319, 384, 409, 415-6

POLAND
    382, 444

POLICY
    275

POLITICS OF FOOD
  see food and politics

POPULATION
    18, 68

PORTUGAL
    192, 363

PRICE POLICY
    13, 19, 40, 46, 47, 56, 72, 88, 98, 129, 141, 158, 164, 171, 213, 226, 228, 271
  cereals
    6, 148, 149, 216, 266

PRICE SUPPORT
    5, 100, 166, 233, 237, 257

PRIVATE TRADE AGREEMENTS
    367, 384, 388, 404, 409, 410, 412-415

PUBLIC LAW 480
  also see Food for Peace
    10, 30, 33, 35 37, 47, 53, 78, 79, 88, 93, 99, 100, 105, 106, 112, 144, 146, 148, 149, 151, 158, 207, 221, 228, 232, 248, 250, 251, 253, 257, 258, 264, 266, 269, 270, 281, 296, 302, 305, 306, 307, 308, 310, 312, 313, 314, 315, 316, 318, 320, 323, 328, 336, 341, 342, 343, 344, 345, 348, 354, 358, 360, 361, 363, 365, 366, 368-72, 377, 381, 383, 387, 390, 391, 395, 398, 409-418, 429, 430
annual reports
    363, 369, 371, 372, 409-418
barter program
    298, 410, 411, 412
budgeting
    299, 300, 301, 302, 303, 322, 333, 349, 350-51, 403
research
    3, 10, 49, 76, 382, 409
Title I
    3, 10, 14, 296, 363, 369, 376, 377, 380-1, 384, 389, 402-4, 409-418
Title II
    4, 30, 296, 363, 380, 385, 402, 410-18
Title III
    32, 358, 380, 402
Title IV
    367, 388
transition to dollar sales
    381, 385, 410

QUATAR
    51

SAHEL
    6, 14, 165, 205, 235, 263, 304, 311, 317, 354

SAUDI ARABIA
    51

· SENEGAL
    15, 304

SIERRA LEONE
    142, 143, 384, 410, 412

SOMALI REPUBLIC
    410, 412

SOUTH AFRICA
    109

SOUTH AMERICA
    69

SOUTH KOREA
    108

SOUTH VIETNAM
    see Vietnam
    222

SOVIET UNION
    see Union of Soviet Socialist
    Republics

SPAIN
    193, 388

SRI LANKA
    96, 244, 319, 363

SUDAN
    254, 304, 417

SWEDEN
    194, 210

SWITZERLAND
    50, 195, 249

SYRIA
    305, 363

TAIWAN
    146, 287, 410, 412

TANZANIA
    125, 147, 154, 304, 363, 432

TECHNICAL ASSISTANCE
    36, 67, 443

THAILAND
    119, 319, 327

TOBACCO
    298

TOGO
    42

TUNISIA
    35, 204, 272, 363, 384,
    409, 410, 412, 416, 429

TURKEY
    196, 267

UGANDA
    309

UNION OF SOVIET SOCIALIST REPUBLICS
    89, 95, 108, 224, 335, 374

UNITED ARAB EMIRATES
    51, 267

UNITED KINGDOM
    90, 108, 122, 197, 251

UNITED NATIONS
    222

UNITED STATES OF AMERICA
    198, 210, 220, 222, 223,
    225, 231, 238, 246, 425
    food aid programs (see Food
    for Peace and Public Law 480)

UPPER VOLTA
    15, 42, 272, 273, 304

URUGUAY
    58, 410, 412

USUAL MARKETING REQUIREMENT
    99

VENEZUELA
    29, 58

VIETMAN
    299, 345, 366, 384, 386,
    387, 409, 410, 412, 413,
    414, 415, 416, 417, 418

VOLUNTARY AGENCIES
    30, 312, 315

WEST BANK
   305

WHEAT EXPORTERS
   99

WORLD BANK
   262, 276, 294, 433

WORLD FOOD CONFERENCE
   220, 261, 263, 276, 321, 338,
   339, 434

WORLD FOOD COUNCIL
   260, 293, 338, 364, 393, 407
   425

WORLD FOOD PROBLEM
   1, 17, 35, 60, 61, 80, 102, 111,
   121, 138, 139, 150, 167, 225,
   239, 251, 261, 263, 280, 281,
   353, 355, 406, 427

WORLD FOOD PROGRAM
   255, 256, 282, 300, 343, 363,
   406, 407, 411, 416, 417, 435-442

YUGOSLAVIA
   199

ZAIRE
   409, 410, 412, 415, 416

ZAMBIA
   46

LIST OF ABBREVIATIONS

AID	Agency for International Development (United States)
ARPAC	United States Agricultural Research Political Advisory Committee
CAP	Common Agricultural Policy
CARE	Co-operative for American Relief Everywhere
CCC	Commodity Credit Corporation (United States)
CDC	Commonwealth Development Corporation
CFA	Committee on Food Aid Policies and Programs (WFP)
CSB	Corn Soya Blend
CSD	Consultative Sub-committee on Surplus Disposal
CSM	Corn Soya Milk
DAC	Development Assistance Committee (OECD)
DC/DCS	Developed Country/ies
EC/EEC	European Economic Community
ERS	Economic Research Service (USDA)
FAC	Food Aid Convention
FAS	Foreign Agricultural Service (USDA)
FAO	United Nations Food and Agriculture Organization
GATT	General Agreement on Tariffs and Trade
GPO	United States Government Printing Office
IBRD	International Bank for Reconstruction and Development (World Bank)
IFAD	International Fund for Agricultural Development
IFPRI	International Food Policy Research Institute
ILO	International Labour Organization
IMF	International Monetary Fund
LDC	Less Developed Country

NGO	Non-governmental Organization
NTIS	National Technical Information Service (United States)
ODC	Overseas Development Council
ODI	Overseas Development Institute
OECD	Organization for Economic Co-operation and Development
P.L. or PL 480	Public Law 480
UK	United Kingdom
UMR	Usual Marketing Requirement
UN	United Nations
UNCTAD	United Nations Conference on Trade and Development
USAID	United States Agency for International Development
USDA	United States Department of Agriculture
WFP	World Food Programme
WHO	World Health Organization